of Congress Cataloging-in-Publication Data:

 Heather.
hy moats matter : the Morningstar approach to stock investing / Heather Brilliant, Elizabeth Collins.
1 online resource.
ludes index.
scription based on print version record and CIP data provided by publisher; resource not
ed.
3N 978-1-118-76102-1 (pdf) — ISBN 978-1-118-76027-7 (epub) —
3N 978-1-118-76023-9 (hardback)
1. Stocks.   2. Investment analysis.   I. Collins, Elizabeth, 1979-   II. Morningstar, Inc.
tle.
61
3'22—dc23
                                                                    2014017196

n the United States of America.
7 6 5 4 3 2 1

W9-BIE-985

Bob Bailey
August 2014

Notes

1. look for a Narrow or wide moat
2. Look for FMV us price
3. Look at moat trend

Why Moo

Matter

The Mor
to Stock

OTHER

1. Check UG health care
2. Sell some P&G? Neg moat.
3. Avoid UPS. Losing share to
3. XOM, TOT, Chevron: neg m

Heather Brilliant
and Elizabeth Collins

WILEY

Jacke

Copy
Publi
Publi

No p
form
exce
eith
app
019
Pub
Inc.
ww

Lin
eff
ac
wa
or
cc
w
o
d

F
c
S

This book is dedicated to Morningstar's equity analysts,
past, present, and future.

Contents

Preface

Finding great businesses at great prices is the holy grail of investing. Yet surprisingly few investors focus on uncovering businesses with the potential to compound in value over time. Why is this? For one thing, uncovering the next Coca-Cola or Johnson & Johnson is hard—these great businesses are much more identifiable after they have been pumping out fantastic returns for years. Further, many assume that the greatness of these businesses must already be well-understood by the market, and therefore trade at prices that already reflect all the benefits of owning them. But that's not always the case—not by a long shot. In this book, we lay out a framework for finding great businesses, and show you how to know when they're trading at a discount to intrinsic value. These concepts form the cornerstone of Morningstar's approach to stock investing.

At Morningstar, we've always viewed investing in the most fundamental sense: We want to hold shares in great businesses for long periods of time. How can you tell a great business from a poor one? A great business is one that can fend off competition and earn high returns on capital for many years to come. Clearly, anyone can look at the historical returns a business has earned to see whether it has benefited from a competitive advantage in the past—but our goal is to find businesses with the potential to keep generating excess returns in the future. To do that, we need to understand how the business generates cash flow. We do this by examining the competitive landscape of the industry and focusing on how a given company competes within that industry. We're looking for companies that have economic moats—structural advantages that protect them from competitors, just as physical moats protected castles from enemies. Through our research, we've determined that economic moats generally stem from at least one of five sources of competitive advantage—cost advantage, intangible assets, switching costs, efficient scale, and network effect—each of which we explore in great depth throughout this book.

Even better than finding a great business is finding one at a great price. The stock market affords virtually unlimited opportunities to track prices and buy or sell securities at any hour of the day or night. But looking past that noise and understanding the value of a business' underlying cash flows is the key to successful long-term investing. When you focus on a company's fundamental value relative to its stock price, and not where the stock price sits today versus a month ago, a day ago, or five minutes ago, you start to think like an owner, not a trader. And thinking like an owner will make you a better investor. We walk you through our approach to valuing businesses, which focuses on estimating the cash we expect a business to generate in the future, and discounting that to the present in order to arrive at a fair value estimate for the business.

As you've probably guessed, this book doesn't tell you how to get rich quick by juggling stocks. What it gives you is a fundamental framework for successful long-term investing. The book will help you answer two key questions: How can I identify a great business, and when should I buy that business to maximize my return? If you get these two things right more often than not, you're well on your way to investing success.

Ours is not the only valid method for investing in stocks, but it's one that has worked well over the years. Using fundamental moat and valuation analysis has led to superior risk-adjusted returns and made Morningstar analysts some of the industry's top stock-pickers. In this book, we share all the ins and outs of our moat-driven investment philosophy, which you can use to identify great stock picks for your own portfolio.

Acknowledgments

Morningstar's entire global equity research team contributed to this book, and we're fortunate to have such a great group working together every day to analyze companies and competitive advantage. Mike Holt, Joel Bloomer, and Alex Morozov have each done a fantastic job leading the team from Chicago, Sydney, and Amsterdam, respectively, and we're very appreciative of their help and support in putting this book together. We would also like to specifically thank those members of the team who contributed chapters to *Why Moats Matter*. We have Stephen Ellis to thank for an extremely well-written analysis of moat trends in Chapter 3. Chapter 4 on stewardship, a critical element in long-term investing, was contributed by Todd Wenning. Chapter 5 delves into dividends and how moats relate to choosing strong dividend-paying companies, thanks to our in-house dividend expert Josh Peters. Joel Bloomer, Matt Coffina, and Gareth James all contributed to Chapter 6 on valuation, which is a critical component of how we think about stocks and investing at Morningstar. This book would not be complete without a thorough statistical analysis around when our investing philosophy works well, and Warren Miller, head of quantitative research, goes through this in great detail in Chapter 7.

The second half of our book, addressing how to analyze moats across sectors, was quite literally made possible by the contributions of our global sector teams. Every analyst on our global team contributed to these chapters through their coverage of companies, the industry research they have written, and their participation in twice-weekly moat committee meetings to debate the application of our economic moat framework and philosophy. We distilled a decade's worth of knowledge and experience around analyzing moats into industry-level moat frameworks, to help investors better apply the economic moat concept to specific investment ideas. A special thanks to the heads of the sector teams, Damien Conover, Stephen Ellis, Adam Fleck, R.J. Hottovy, Travis Miller, Alex Morozov, Keith Schoonmaker, Jim Sinegal, Jason Stevens, and Peter Wahlstrom, for their support and contributions to this section.

This book could not have happened without the help of Catherine Sanders and Kailee Kremer, both of whose extensive edits enhanced the readability and cohesiveness of the text. Chris Cantore designed our cover, and both Chris and Barbara Kennedy designed every last chart, table, and graphic in the book. Special thanks go to Lauren Adams for her efforts to keep every one of us moving on this important project. Lauren kept the process organized and focused on the end goal.

Finally, we would like to thank Joe Mansueto, Haywood Kelly, Catherine Odelbo, and Don Phillips, who have been strong advocates for Morningstar's equity research department since its earliest days.

Guiding Principles of Morningstar's Equity Research

What is a moat? For most people, images of water-filled trenches protecting castles from invaders immediately come to mind. We have taken that concept and applied it to investing, where an economic moat is a structural barrier protecting companies from competition.

Here at Morningstar, we've always viewed investing in the most fundamental sense of the word: We want to hold shares in great businesses for long periods of time. So what's a great business? Essentially, we believe it's one that can fend off competition and earn high returns on capital for many years into the future—increasing earnings, returning cash to shareholders, and compounding intrinsic value. Identifying companies like this is the goal of our economic moat analysis and our Morningstar Economic Moat Rating, which we explore in great detail in the coming chapters.

Even better than finding a great business is finding one at a great price. The stock market affords virtually unlimited opportunities to track prices and buy or sell securities at any hour of the day or night, but we think the key to successful long-term investing is concentrating not on the daily price movements of a stock but on the value of the cash flows generated by the underlying business. When you focus on a company's underlying fundamental value relative to its stock price, and not where the stock price is today relative to a month ago or a day ago or five minutes ago, you start to think like an owner, rather than a trader.

If you're looking for a book on how to get rich quick by trading in the stock market, you've come to the wrong place. Our goal is to give you a fundamental framework for successful long-term investing, which, we admit, is all we really know how to do. Our book aims to answer two primary questions: How can we identify which businesses are great? And when is the best time to buy these businesses, in order to maximize potential returns? If you can get just these two things right more often than not, you'll be well on your way to becoming a successful long-term investor.

When Morningstar first started analyzing stocks more than a decade ago, we began with some core principles that guide our research to this day. Then and now, our analytic work has centered on three main elements: sustainable competitive advantages, valuation, and margin of safety, which we believe are the keys to outperforming the stock market over time. How exactly do we define these terms and why do they matter? That's the purpose of this book. Throughout the coming chapters, we give you an overview of each of these principles, with the primary focus on how to identify companies with sustainable competitive advantages, or economic moats.

Question 1: How Can We Identify Which Businesses Are Great?

The answer to this question lies in finding companies with sustainable competitive advantages, or economic moats. Just as moats were dug around medieval castles to keep enemies at bay, economic moats protect the high returns on capital enjoyed by the world's best companies.

Moats

In a famous 1999 *Fortune* article, legendary investor Warren Buffett wrote, "The key to investing is . . . determining the competitive advantage of any given company and, above all, the durability of that advantage. The products or services that have wide, sustainable moats around them are the ones that deliver rewards to investors." With gratitude to Mr. Buffett, Morningstar has taken the economic moat concept a step further and developed a comprehensive moat-based analytic framework that can be applied consistently across a broad, global list of companies.

Whenever a company develops a profitable product or service, it isn't long before other firms try to capitalize on that opportunity by producing a similar version, or even improving on the original version. We know from microeconomics that in a perfectly competitive market, rivals will eventually compete away any excess profits earned by a successful business. Nokia boasted the majority share of the mobile phone market for several years, but the introduction of Apple's iPhone in 2007 and the subsequent evolution of the smartphone market left the flat-footed Nokia behind. A similar shift has occurred in the gaming industry, where longtime powerhouse Nintendo is seeing its iconic, family-friendly franchises left behind by powerful new consoles boasting high-end third-party software, such as Microsoft's Xbox and Sony's PlayStation. Meanwhile, mobile devices have begun to erode Nintendo's dominant position in the handheld gaming market. In other words, profits attract competitors, and competition makes it difficult for firms to generate strong growth and margins over the long term.

But there are definitely some companies that manage to earn high returns on capital for extended periods of time. These companies are able to withstand the relentless onslaught of competition for long stretches, and these are the wealth-compounding machines that we want to find and own.

It's important to note that an economic moat must be a structural element of the business itself. We're not looking for companies with better short-term execution than competitors, or cyclical improvements that make returns on capital look good. We're looking for companies where the business and industry structure protect profits. Along these lines, while great management can certainly enhance a company's moat, just as poor management can detract from it, management itself cannot form the basis of an economic moat (more on that in Chapter 4).

Moats and Value Creation

How much value a company will create for itself and its shareholders depends on two things: the amount of value currently being created and the business' ability to continue to create value well into the future. The first factor is widely

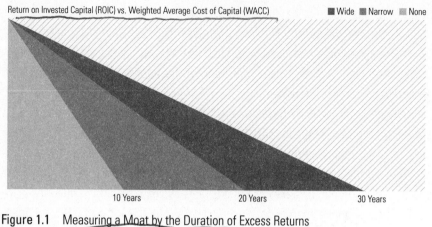

Figure 1.1   Measuring a Moat by the Duration of Excess Returns
Source: Morningstar.

known by the market because it's easy to calculate using basic financial statements. It's the second factor, the magnitude and duration of future excess returns, that is harder to determine but is ultimately more important for successful long-term investing.

Here's another way to illustrate this idea: Take three companies, each with a similar value-creating return on invested capital, or ROIC, today. The company that is able to sustain those excess returns the longest is going to be able to add the most value for itself over the coming years. In Figure 1.1, the company with the widest moat and the longest advantage period has the greatest value creation (area under the curve).

Moats in Action

What does an economic moat look like for a real live company? Take electric utility ITC Holdings as an example. Electricity transmission isn't exactly a sexy business, but investors in this pure-play transmission company have enjoyed double-digit earnings growth and healthy returns on capital thanks to its dominant market position and favorable long-term regulatory framework. We believe this "boring" utility has a wide economic moat that should protect those high returns for years to come. Its competitors have little incentive to build competing transmission lines if one that ITC owns is already serving a market's full capacity; capital costs are too high and incremental benefits too low to offer sufficient returns for two competing transmission owners. In addition, ITC benefits from regulatory protection. The Federal Energy Regulatory Commission approves new transmission lines only if there is a demonstrated need for new capacity. In exchange for regulatory protection, ITC must charge rates based on a formula that allows ITC to recover its expenses and earn a reasonable return on investment. We believe that because of its transparency and predictability, a forward-looking formula rate—which is more investor-friendly than typical backward-looking rates given to most utilities—results in a below-average cost of capital for ITC and supports stable cash returns that we expect to last years into the future.

Contrast this with no-moat ethanol firms like Pacific Ethanol, VeraSun Energy, and Aventine Renewable Energy that boomed and then quickly busted in the past decade. The ethanol frenzy rose to a fever pitch in mid-2006, fueled by waves of government support and hotly anticipated IPOs. Two years later, investors in the corn-based fuel product were left with billions of dollars in losses as lofty expectations of this "wonder product" failed to pan out. This disappointment exemplifies an industry where it's virtually impossible for a company to earn a moat, while it's easy for new ethanol firms to enter, and hard for any single firm to establish a cost advantage, causing eventual oversupply and weak or nonexistent profits for all players.

Moat Sources

Over years of studying companies, we have identified five major sources of competitive advantage, or economic moat. We discuss each source in depth in the next chapter, but here's a quick rundown of the five:

1. Intangible assets

     Intangible assets include brands, patents, or government licenses that explicitly keep competitors at bay.

2. Cost advantage

     Firms that have the ability to provide goods or services at lower cost have an advantage because they can undercut their rivals on price. Alternatively, they may sell their products or services at the same prices as rivals, but achieve fatter profit margins. We consider economies of scale to be a type of cost advantage, an idea we discuss in more detail in the next chapter.

3. Switching costs

Switching costs are those one-time inconveniences or expenses a customer incurs to change from one product to another. Customers facing high
switching costs often won't change providers unless they are offered a large
improvement in either price or performance, and even then, the risk associated with making a change may still prevent switching in some industries.

4. Network effect

The network effect occurs when the value of a particular good or service increases for both new and existing users as more people use that
good or service, often creating a viscious circle that allows strong companies to become even stronger.

5. Efficient scale

Efficient scale describes a dynamic in which a market of limited size is
effectively served by one or just a few companies. The companies involved
generate economic profits, but potential competitors are discouraged from
entering because doing so would result in insufficient returns for all players.

Assigning Moat Ratings

When assigning moat ratings, we first consider the five qualitative factors outlined earlier. But we also look for quantitative evidence of a moat, namely, a company's ability to earn excess returns on invested capital. The size of the spread
between ROIC and cost of capital is actually far less important than the expected
duration of the excess profits. When we believe that a company will more likely
than not benefit from a competitive advantage and earn excess returns for a
period of at least 10 years, we assign it a narrow moat rating. When we're near-
certain that a firm will earn excess returns for the next 10 years, and likely for the
next 20 years, we assign the firm a wide moat rating. Clearly, the hurdle is high
for earning a wide moat rating, and despite scouring the universe of listed companies, we have assigned wide moat ratings to fewer than 200 companies globally.

Question 2: When Is the Best Time to Invest in Great Businesses?

It's tempting to conclude that wide-moat businesses are so rare and so great
that you should buy them whenever you find them and hold on to them as

long as their competitive advantages remain intact. However, the competitive advantage of a business is only part of the story. Our research shows that while wide moats can be a tremendous source of alpha, or excess return, for your portfolio, the advantage of owning wide-moat companies is much clearer and more persistent when you purchase them at a discount to the underlying business value.

The Importance of Valuation

Valuation is an incredibly important aspect of investing—you could argue, *the* most important. It makes sense when you think about it: You wouldn't want to pay $650,000 for a house that's worth $500,000, because even if it were a great house, it would take many years for the market to recognize the value of the house as $650,000, and at that point, you would have likely lost purchasing power in real terms after inflation. Even if you bought that same house for $500,000, or fair market value, you would see it appreciate only at the market rate of return. Ideally, you'd get an even better price on the house, perhaps buying it for $450,000, so you could benefit not only from the future market rate of return, but also from having the price converge from your discounted price to the fair market value.

While many investors get caught up in daily stock price movements, we prefer to think about valuation in the same way as you would a real asset, such as the house in the example above. There is a fair market value of any business, and opportunities to purchase great businesses at less than that fair market value give investors an advantage in generating future returns.

Estimating Fair Value

The key to successfully purchasing an asset at a discount to fair market value is accurately estimating the future cash flows you expect that business to generate. This is no easy feat, and there are many different ways to go about it. Some analysts look at current cash flows, or even earnings, as a proxy for cash flow, and assign a multiple to that earnings number to roughly "guesstimate" how long into the future they expect that cash-flow level and growth rate to persist. Others assume a perpetual growth rate, such as a long-term estimate of inflation, and use that to calculate the company's expected cash flows into perpetuity, then discount those cash flows back to a present-day figure.

At Morningstar, in an effort to be as precise as possible, we take a funda-mental approach to valuation analysis and build a discounted cash-flow model for each company we cover. We talk through the details of that in Chapter 5, but in the meantime, here's a quick summary of what that means. After researching the company and its industry, we explicitly estimate the firm's revenue, earn-ings, balance sheet, and cash generation for the next several years (five to 10 years, depending on the situation). Consistent with microeconomic theory, we assume all businesses will earn their cost of capital only in the long run as competitors eat away at any excess returns—but we assume companies with wide moats will benefit from longer periods of excess returns than those with narrow moats, which will still earn excess returns for longer periods than busi-nesses without moats. Then we discount the future cash flows back to the pres-ent using the firm's estimated cost of capital.

There are many points of uncertainty in this process, so we take a few extra steps to strengthen our analysis and adjust for potential unknown (and sometimes unknowable) factors. First, we put a lot of emphasis on scenario analysis, or looking at what the company would be worth in various situations. It's important to recognize that no one actually knows the exact fair market value of any business, so the goal is to understand the range of possible out-comes and narrow that range whenever possible. Second, we always look for a margin of safety before investing, even in a wide-moat company.

Margin of Safety

The concept of margin of safety has been around for decades; legendary value investors such as Ben Graham, Warren Buffett, and Seth Klarman have writ-ten about and utilized margin of safety in their investing disciplines. The basic idea is that because no one knows the true value of a security, purchasing it at materially less than fair value will help improve your odds of making a success-ful investment, because even if it's worth less than you originally estimated, you have improved your chances of a positive return by buying it at a discount.

Not every company requires the same margin of safety, though, and understanding how to adjust the discount you require can put the odds in your favor. Because of this, we developed the Morningstar Uncertainty Rating to help clearly identify the discount (or premium) we would seek before recom-mending the purchase (or sale) of a stock. We think uncertainty largely boils down to how difficult it is to forecast the future cash flows of the business in question. To try to gauge this, we look at the variability in revenues, operating income, and financial leverage over the course of economic cycles, as well as company-specific risks, because the cash flows of a business with wide swings in revenue, high fixed costs, and lots of debt, such as cement maker Cemex, are much harder to forecast than those of a very steady, conservatively run business like food giant Nestle.

That's a quick overview of our stock research process: look for a moat, determine a fair value, and leave room for error. Easier said than done. The following chapters delve more deeply into each of these topics and teach you how you can tackle each of these problems using the same tools and techniques we use when we're analyzing stocks at Morningstar.

In Chapter 2, we explore the five sources of economic moat in detail. Here and throughout the book, we use specific company examples to help illustrate how we think about moats and valuation in real-world situations. Chapter 3 focuses on moat trends, which provide perspective on how moats grow and shrink over time—moat trends provide a more dynamic assessment of how a company's competitive position is evolving. Chapters 4 and 5 elaborate on how to incorporate management and stewardship into the evaluation of a company's moat, with a particular focus on capital allocation and dividends.

We turn next to our valuation methodology, to give you a glimpse into our discounted cash-flow process and how we use it to estimate the intrinsic value of a business. In this section, we also include a few real-world portfolio examples, so you can see how we put moats, valuation, and margin of safety into practice.

Think of the second half of the book as a how-to guide for analyzing moats in each sector. We walk through each sector in detail, so you can understand how the evaluation of a firm's competitive advantage relates to its industry, get some perspective on how moats differ by sector, and gain tools to analyze a company's moat.

Throughout this book, we share the details behind our investment philosophy and our approach to company analysis. Our goal is to provide you with the methods to determine a company's moat, fair value, and margin of safety so you can apply this approach to your own investment decision-making.

2

What Makes a Moat?

Now that you have the big picture of what we mean by *economic moat* and why we think it's so important for successful stock investing, let's get into the details of how we define and identify moats for individual companies.

To determine a company's economic moat rating, we start by asking two questions:

1. Are the company's returns on invested capital, or ROIC, likely to exceed its weighted average cost of capital, or WACC, in the future?[1]
2. Does the company appear to have at least one of the five sources of sustainable competitive advantage (intangible assets, cost advantage, switching costs, network effect, or efficient scale)?

In this regard, our moat methodology considers both quantitative and qualitative factors—the ROIC-WACC spread, also referred to as *economic profits*, and the moat sources, respectively. A firm generates economic profits when its earnings exceed not only accounting costs but also investors' opportunity costs. A firm can generate positive net income, or positive accounting profits, without posting economic profits if it doesn't reward equity investors for putting their money in the business.

The process of answering these fundamental questions about future economic profits and sustainable competitive advantages includes carefully researching the company and its industry. At Morningstar, our process includes analyzing the company's financial statements, talking to its managers, visiting the firm's operations when relevant, and reading industry publications. This fundamental analysis is a key component of understanding the outlook for a company's future profitability and competitive forces. If we think ROICs are likely to exceed WACC in the future, and the company appears to have any of the five sources of competitive advantage, it's possible that the firm does indeed have a narrow or wide economic moat. But the investigation doesn't stop there. We next assess the company's ability to generate positive economic profits 10 to 20 years into the future. In free-market economies, rivals will eventually encroach on any excess profits earned by companies without protective moats—time and capital requirements aren't effective barriers to entry when we have a long-term time horizon. Some companies may generate positive ROIC-WACC spreads today and for a few years into the future. But if their competitive advantages aren't sustainable enough, competitors will begin to eat into excess profits over time.

Therefore, for a company to earn our narrow economic moat rating, we must find evidence that at least one source of competitive advantage exists and that economic profits will be positive for at least 10 years. If we think economic profits will endure for at least 20 years, the firm earns our wide moat rating. We believe sustainability is much more important than the magnitude of economic profits when assessing economic moats. In other words, a highly certain 20-year stream of modest economic profits is much more moatworthy than a few years of extraordinarily high returns on invested capital. The 10- and 20-year benchmarks are somewhat arbitrary, but the idea is to focus on the long-term cash generation potential of the underlying business and put some parameters around approximately how long we expect excess returns to last. It's also important to note that we're considering economic profits in a normalized, or "midcycle," environment. If we expect a company to generate robust ROICs only during peak industry conditions, then it's not a candidate for our narrow or wide moat ratings. On the flip side, if a company isn't earning economic (or even accounting) profits today because it's in the depths of an industry trough or because extraordinary one-time factors are at play, it's not precluded from earning a narrow or wide moat rating.

Note that our moat-rating methodology is absolute, not relative. We're simply looking for companies that have (1) sustainable competitive advantages and (2) a likelihood of generating positive economic profits for a decade or more. Narrow and wide moat ratings are not reserved for only the best companies in a given industry, and some industries may lack any companies with sustainable competitive advantages at all. To ensure we apply our methodology consistently across our broad coverage universe, and given the central importance of the economic moat rating to the Morningstar equity research methodology, a committee of 15 senior members of the Morningstar research team oversees all of the individual company ratings. Because the committee members represent each of the major sectors, this approach provides context for an individual company's rating, and we can avoid common pitfalls such as thinking that only the finest company in an industry deserves a wide moat, or that "best-in-industry" status automatically equates to a sustainable competitive advantage.

Moat Sources

Now we're ready to dig into the moat sources one by one. For each of the five sources we provide lists of critical questions that you can ask yourself when determining whether a particular company has a narrow or wide economic moat. If you've read even a handful of 10-K annual reports, you know that most companies present a list of competitive advantages that sound moatworthy, such as patents, brands, cost advantages, and strong customer relationships. The questions we have assembled are designed to help ferret out whether a company truly benefits from one of the moat sources. Further, in our years of reading 10-Ks, we've found it rare for companies to explicitly mention advantages such as switching costs, network effect, or efficient scale. So, finding companies with these sources requires an extra level of analysis, and these key questions are meant to help you uncover companies with these powerful sources. For each source, we provide a few examples, so you can see how these play out in the real world.

Intangible Assets

Intangible assets is a broad category that includes brands, patents, and regulatory licenses.

Brands A brand creates an economic moat around a company's profits if it increases the customer's willingness to pay or increases customer captivity. A moatworthy brand manifests itself as pricing power or repeat business that translates into sustainable economic profits.

Key Questions: Brands

1. **How do you quantify the strength of the brand? What is the pricing power that the brand conveys? What is the premium that the company can charge relative to competitors?** High name recognition doesn't always translate into pricing power. Just think of airlines such as United or American—you're probably very aware of these brands, but that doesn't mean you're willing to pay more for a United or American ticket. Most likely you'll make your purchasing decision based solely on cost after factoring in class, mileage credits, and baggage fees, and we see this reflected in the poor returns these airlines generate. As a result, most airlines lack sustainable competitive advantages.
2. **Is the premium offset by higher costs?** Some companies do indeed charge higher prices than their competitors, but that merely reflects a higher cost of production. For a brand to be moatworthy, it must confer pricing power that at least offsets any difference in costs.
3. **How do the company's margins compare with competitors that don't have strong brands?** If you don't have specific data on prices and costs, you can look at a company's profit margins relative to its peers for signs of pricing power.
4. **What gives you confidence that the brand strength, the premium pricing, and the higher operating margins are sustainable**

for 10–20 years? Brands come and go, and sustainability is the most important factor when determining economic moats. After all, history is littered with examples of well-recognized brands that didn't lead to sustainable returns, such as Crocs, Nokia, and Palm. Although it's hard to predict which brands will remain powerful decades into the future, companies that continuously plow money into innovation and marketing are more likely to have powerful brands in the future. Further, lifelong brands arguably have more longevity potential than companies with high-turnover client bases. For example, once a consumer develops a taste for, say, Coke over Pepsi, that's a preference that will likely hold, and Coca-Cola can rely on having the same customer for decades. However, new parents deciding on infant formula develop a brand preference that lasts only during the early child-rearing years, and therefore formula companies such as Mead Johnson must constantly acquire cohorts of new parents.

Walt Disney   Walt Disney is a good example of a company that has built a moat based on the intangible asset of brand. In fact, strong brands support robust and sustainable economic profits at both of Walt Disney's key businesses: cable networks and Disney-branded businesses (parks, filmed entertainment, and consumer products). On the cable side of the business, strong networks like ESPN earn rich subscriber fees and profits. These profits allow the company to spend on long-term programming rights with the major professional sports leagues and college athletic conferences, which reinforces ESPN's position as the leader in its category. The strength of this brand has allowed the company to expand the franchise and has resulted in several sister channels and the most popular website dedicated to sports content. In the Disney-branded businesses, the company exploits strong characters and franchises across multiple platforms. Disney has been creating high-quality family entertainment for decades and has become a brand that children seek and parents trust. Disney's theme parks and resorts are difficult for competitors to replicate, especially considering the tie-ins with its other business lines. A Disney character franchise typically starts with a theatrical release, but can be further exploited through DVD sales, licensing to television networks, sequels, merchandising, and theme park attractions. Each new successful franchise becomes a valuable addition to Disney's large library of content, which can be monetized for decades.

Starbucks Starbucks remains the dominant player in specialty coffee, and its brand commands premium pricing for what is truly a commodity. Coffee is a globally fungible commodity (in other words, it is easily replaced by another identical product) that is traded on liquid exchanges with complete price transparency. Still, Starbucks' customers are willing to fork over extra dollars for a cup with a green mermaid, thanks to the experience Starbucks has created as part of its brand. As a result, we expect Starbucks to generate handsome economic profits in the coming decades, with ROICs in excess of 20% over the long term.

BMW Bayerische Motoren Werke AG earns our narrow moat rating, thanks to the strength and global recognition of its brands, its technological leadership in powertrain, its ability to command premium pricing from consumers that regularly rate its vehicles as some of the best to own, and its ability to consistently generate excess returns. Even though the venerable Rolls-Royce and BMW brand names command premium pricing, consumers can easily switch to other brands, like Bentley or Audi, and a seemingly bulletproof brand image can tarnish quickly. However, thanks to an ingrained culture that obsesses over the details that the company's customers demand, we think BMW will continue to successfully manage its brand images—ranging from premium-priced BMW motorcycles and Cooper MINI passenger cars, to luxury BMW passenger cars and crossovers, to ultraluxury Rolls-Royce cars—leading to economic value creation for investors. The company's returns exceeded its cost of capital in 10 of the past 11 years, an outstanding performance for an automotive manufacturer and a phenomenon that we expect will endure.

Patents Sometimes patents are a source of sustainable competitive advantage for a company, although not all patents lead to narrow or wide economic moat ratings. If patents protect a company's main products, and there are no viable alternatives, then the company may have pricing power for a sustained period while other industry players are legally barred from competing.

Key Questions: Patents

1. **What is the expiration schedule for the company's patent portfolio?** Because a narrow or wide economic moat rating depends on a company's ability to produce economic profits for a decade or more, patents that expire within the next several years certainly don't confer a moat by themselves.
2. **How diverse is the company's patent portfolio?** A company with a wider breadth of patented products is more likely to have a narrow or wide moat because the diversity leads to higher chances that the company will generate economic profits for a decade or more. A company with a history of successful research and development investment in its patent portfolio is more likely to maintain a patent-related competitive advantage than one without such a track record.
3. **What is the market potential of patentable products in the pipeline and the probability of their success?** Since we need to assess a company's economic-profit-generating potential 10–20 years in the future, we need to analyze the earning potential of products that haven't even come to market yet.
4. **Once products come off patent, how easy will it be for competitors to enter the market?** Sometimes, even when a product comes off patent, competitors will hesitate to enter the market because of the difficulty involved in replicating the offering. For example, generic pressure for biologic drug manufacturers isn't as severe as for traditional pharmaceuticals because of manufacturing difficulties and the costs of clinical trials and product marketing.
5. **What are the potential substitutes for the patented product?** Even a patented product won't garner moatworthy pricing power

(Continued)

(*Continued*)

if effective substitutes are readily available. In markets where patents can more easily be innovated around, such as in the technology or industrials sectors, patents become a less important driver of moats.

6. **How strong is intellectual property protection in the relevant markets?** If patents don't actually keep competitors at bay because of lax intellectual property protections in the markets a company serves, then pricing power is diminished and patents alone are unlikely to convey a sustainable competitive advantage.

Sanofi Like other highly successful pharmaceutical companies, Sanofi benefits from patent protection that keeps competitors at bay for several years while the company charges prices that enable returns on invested capital significantly above its cost of capital. Also, Sanofi's unique entrenched position in the insulin market further reduces the threat of generic competition even after patents expire thanks to the high up-front costs needed to achieve the economies of scale for low-cost insulin production. Sanofi's existing product line boasts several top-tier drugs, including long-acting insulin Lantus. The drug's ability to work well for an entire day sets Lantus apart from other insulins. Given the complexity in marketing and manufacturing insulin, we don't expect major generic competition following the drug's 2015 patent loss. The company's leadership in the insulin and rare-disease biologic markets exposes Sanofi to less-pronounced generic threats; we believe eventual generic competition will not destroy branded sales to the same extent that we see with generic small molecules, given the marketing and manufacturing complexity associated with biologic drugs. Further, Sanofi has compiled a robust group of late-stage pipeline products that complement its existing lineup and should help mitigate patent losses.

iRobot A patent portfolio worth mentioning belongs to iRobot, maker of Roomba (the robotic vacuum cleaner) as well as military and police robots. The company has a perceived product advantage that is backed by strong patent protection. Outside Korea, where players such as Samsung and LG have found success with their own high-end products, iRobot has not faced meaningful competition in its home robot division, even as the company has sold more than 6 million Roombas worldwide. We attribute this success to a continued strong patent portfolio; the only competing products have been too expensive, of lower quality, or poorly managed, preventing them from denting iRobot's competitive position.

Monsanto Having created the agricultural biotechnology market where it now competes, Monsanto has a wide economic moat. The company's portfolio of patented traits—seed characteristics that improve farmers' profitability—forms the basis of its moat, much in the same way patent-protected drugs form the moat foundation for a pharmaceutical firm. Monsanto's proprietary seeds use the traits it develops, but the firm also licenses traits for use by others. This strategy has led to dominant market share, and Monsanto enjoys premium pricing for its patented traits. Monsanto uses the cash flows generated from its current product lineup to invest in research and development for next-generation offerings. The company consistently pours 10% of sales into R&D each year. Monsanto is also a very attractive partner for agricultural biotech companies without their own extensive seed platforms. Further, the company owns an industry-leading germplasm (a seed bank for conventional and molecular hybrid breeding) and a global breeding operation that are difficult to replicate. Signs of Monsanto's dominance in genetically modified, or GM, seeds are readily apparent, including rivals' accusations of controlling an unfair monopoly and the fact that some competitors choose to license the firm's technology instead of going head-to-head with Monsanto. For example, Syngenta and DuPont have chosen to license Roundup Ready 2 Yield for their second-generation soybean offerings instead of investing the dollars to develop their own platforms. We think Monsanto will earn returns on invested capital above the firm's cost of capital for quite some time.

Regulations Government regulations are another intangible asset that can lead to sustainable competitive advantages if the rules make it difficult or even impossible for competitors to enter the market. Regulations are especially favorable if a company can operate like a monopoly but isn't regulated like one with regard to pricing.

Key Questions: Regulations

1. **Are there offsets to the favorable regulation, such as price controls or service mandates?** Regulatory barriers to entry aren't moatworthy if they come with the burden of price controls or service mandates that prevent economic profit generation. For example, even though Aéroports de Paris has a geographic monopoly on airports serving the number-one tourist destination in the world, the government-regulated rates that ADP can charge for certain services have been too low to allow for economic profit generation.

2. **If regulatory barriers to entry are the key argument, consider the threat of substitutes.** If a company provides a good or service in a particular country and is shielded from competition within the country, consider whether potential customers can meet their needs with goods or services provided by companies from other countries.

3. **What is the most likely outcome for future regulations?** Even if government regulations result in distorted market conditions that differ materially from what would prevail in a more lax regime, we need to base our expectations for future economic profits on the regulatory environment that will most likely prevail.

4. **How material are the risks of adverse regulatory changes?** Our narrow and wide moat ratings require a high degree of confidence in future economic profits. If there's a material chance that regulations will change in a way that depresses future economic profits, this could prevent a company from obtaining our narrow or wide moat rating, depending on the probability and impact of any regulatory change.

Grupo Televisa Grupo Televisa is a good example of a company with a wide economic moat that stems from favorable government regulation. The company generates half of its operating income from its television broadcasting business, where through a licensing arrangement with the Mexican government, Televisa owns and operates many of the leading television networks in the country. If advertisers want to reach Mexican viewers en masse, Televisa is essentially the only way to go. Building on this sustainable competitive advantage in broadcasting, Televisa has amassed a programming empire, and added ownership stakes in cable and satellite TV distribution that give Televisa more than half of Mexico's pay TV market.

Las Vegas Sands and Wynn Resorts Casino operators with Asian facilities, such as Las Vegas Sands and Wynn Resorts, benefit from regulatory barriers to entry, giving Asian casino operators much wider economic moats than their U.S. counterparts. The China market is an oligopoly, with only six licenses granted, and legalized gambling limited to the tiny, densely populated region of Macau; Singapore is a duopoly, with only two licenses. It is extremely unlikely that the Chinese central government will authorize casinos in another province of China, as this would require a change to the Chinese constitution, and Beijing doesn't want gambling to bring societal ills to other provinces in mainland China. Advertising casinos in mainland China is illegal, and Beijing has cracked down hard on illegal gambling. Casino licensing in Macau is quite different than in the United States, in that the companies that receive licenses to operate in Macau are able to open more than one casino, with the limitation that new casinos require government approval and licensed operators must pay an additional fee to the government for each new casino. In the U.S., license holders generally do not have the right to open multiple casinos, and a new license is required for each new casino.

Cost Advantage

Companies can dig economic moats around their businesses by having sustainably lower costs than their competitors. A favorable cost position can stem from process advantages, a superior location, scale, or access to a unique asset. Process advantages are interesting, but we award economic moat ratings to companies with this edge only if the process can't or won't be easily replicated by competitors. An advantageous location can also give a company a cost edge, and this leg up can be sustainable given the difficulty of duplication. Meanwhile, companies that enjoy economies of scale have lower average costs than their competitors with smaller capacities.

Key Questions: Cost Advantage

1. **Does the company benefit from economies of scale? Specifically, which costs are fixed and can therefore be leveraged? What quantitative evidence do we have that this company benefits from lower per-unit costs than a competitor with smaller volumes?** Many companies claim that they benefit from economies of scale, but it's important to look for proof that a company with larger volumes indeed has lower per-unit costs than a smaller competitor.

2. **Does the company benefit from economies of scope?** Which costs are spread over a variety of products? What quantitative evidence demonstrates how this company benefits from lower per-unit costs than a competitor that produces a smaller variety of products? Some companies can leverage significant R&D expenses and process knowledge over a variety of products meeting diverse client needs. Once again, it's crucial to focus on finding actual quantitative support that this results in lower per-unit costs.

3. **Does this company benefit from low transportation costs?** What is the cost of transportation relative to total costs or the price of the product? What is the transportation cost for relevant competitors? Transportation costs can really alter a company's competitive positioning, especially for goods that have a low value/weight ratio. To illustrate, transportation costs matter very little when shipping gold, where an immense amount of value can sit comfortably in the palm of your hand. In contrast, an entire ton of construction aggregates costs only $10. In situations like that, producers located closest to potential customers have a great cost advantage over far-flung competitors.

4. **Does this company own or control geological deposits with advantageous characteristics? How rare or prevalent are deposits of high quality?** In the energy and basic materials sectors, owning an advantaged geological deposit can be a formidable competitive advantage, because humans—even with substantial

capital and time—can't replicate what Mother Nature took millions of years to form.

5. **Does this company have a unique production process that results in a cost advantage? Quantify the cost advantage that comes from this process. Can this process be replicated?** A process-based cost advantage is ultimately replicable, but we do find that some companies can operate for decades with a cost advantage due to a superior production process. Keep an eye out for potential new entrants. While incumbent competitors may be stuck with the inferior production process that they've already built, it's easier for new industry entrants to use a superior production process because they're starting from scratch.

6. **Does this company have bargaining power with suppliers that results in a cost advantage? What percentage of the company's total costs benefits from this bargaining power? What type of discount does this bargaining power result in?** Many companies claim that they're big and powerful enough to extract discounts from their suppliers, but we need to see quantitative proof that this results in a material cost advantage before awarding a narrow or wide economic moat rating on this basis alone. For bargaining power to result in a sustainable competitive advantage, we wouldn't want to see any looming threat of supplier consolidation.

7. **Does this company have advantaged access to raw materials? What percentage of total costs does the raw material amount to? What does the cost advantage amount to, relative to industry competitors that don't have advantaged access to raw materials? Why can't other industry players get access to these low-cost raw materials? What is the outlook for supply, demand, and prices for the raw material?** For example, some companies benefit from having access to low-cost energy. Before considering a narrow or wide moat rating on this basis, though, we need to make sure that the cost advantage is sustainable. Regional changes in supply and demand, or substitution, can cause raw-materials-based advantages to be fleeting.

Managed Care Organizations Managed care organizations, or MCOs, provide a good illustration of the economies-of-scale version of the cost advantage source. These firms provide health insurance services to their members (individuals, groups, or the government). One of the most valuable effects of having a large membership base is that the MCO can significantly scale its selling, general, and administrative, or SG&A, costs. Expenses such as corporate costs, IT infrastructure investments, depreciation of fixed assets, certain selling expenses, payment processing, and customer service expenses are largely fixed, and therefore having more members lowers the average cost per member. The major MCOs that we believe possess economic moats—UnitedHealth, WellPoint, and Aetna—are able to operate at a lower level of SG&A per member than smaller MCOs that don't have moats.

Furthermore, an MCO with a large membership base also has a better ability to control overall medical costs by negotiating advantageous pricing with its providers (hospitals and doctors). To obtain profitable pricing, companies need to either have a large geographic reach to provide demand at multiple nationwide sites or have the local density to control a large portion of demand in a specific geography. Basically, a provider will give better pricing to payers that control more demand. This dynamic is a product of a few factors. First, a procedure usually becomes cheaper to execute for a provider each additional time it is done. Therefore, a provider can cut pricing for a payer with a large membership base and still preserve its gross margins. Second, since a payer that controls a large portion of demand also potentially controls a large portion of a provider's gross profits, the provider will be more apt to provide discounted pricing.

Railroads North American Class I Railroads—CSX, Norfolk Southern, BNSF, Union Pacific, Canadian National, Canadian Pacific, and Kansas City Southern— earn wide economic moats in part from sustainable low-cost advantages. Barges, ships, aircraft, and trucks also haul freight, but railroads are the low-cost option by far where no waterway connects the origin and destination, especially for freight with a low value/weight ratio. Moreover, railroads claim quadruple the fuel efficiency of trucking per ton-mile of freight and make more effective use of manpower despite the need for train-yard personnel, in part because of greater railcar capacity and longer trains. Even for goods that can be shipped by truck, we estimate that railroads charge 10%–30% less than trucking containers on the same lane. And we have confidence in the sustainability of these railroads' economic profits because they've been investing heavily in their cost advantages. They're making increasingly effective use of two of their most expensive inputs: labor and fuel. Regarding the former, railroads are producing more ton-miles per employee than in the past. This is due in part to larger cars, combined with increased speed, reduced downtime at terminals, and more effective work rules and practices. Concerning the latter, the Association of American Railroads reports that in 2012 U.S. railroads moved a ton of freight on average 476 miles per gallon of fuel, up from 414 ton-miles per gallon in 2005 and double the 235 level of 1980. This was accomplished via larger cars, more-fuel-efficient locomotives, idle-reduction technology, throttle position selection guidance software that learns a route to optimize fuel and safety, distributed power to reduce required horsepower, rail lubrication, and locomotive engineer training and incentives.

Switching Costs

Switching costs are the expenses—whether in time, hassle, money, or risk—a customer would incur to change from one producer or provider to another. Customers facing high switching costs won't necessarily make a switch even if a competitor is offering a lower price or a better-performing product or service. The improvement in performance or price must be large enough to offset the cost of switching. High switching costs are especially prevalent and powerful when there is a high cost of failure, or the cost of the specific product or service in question is fairly insignificant relative to the customer's total operating costs.

Key Questions: Switching Costs

1. **What are the costs and benefits of switching?** Comparing the costs of switching with the price differences among available alternatives is the best way to prove that a company benefits from switching costs.
2. **Are customers' existing assets and processes linked to a particular provider's offering?** How material would training

(Continued)

(*Continued*)

needs be if a customer switched providers? How much lead time is necessary for a customer to switch? How significant would the business disruption be if a customer switched providers? Answers to these questions help paint the picture of what switching entails. Sometimes it's hard to quantify switching costs, but high degrees of asset specificity, significant training needs, long lead times, and high potential for business disruption all help create customer switching costs.

3. **What are renewal rates for this company?** High customer switching costs typically manifest themselves in high renewal rates for existing clients.

Apple Apple is a good example of a company whose customers would suffer switching costs if they changed products. There are a variety of switching costs around the iOS platform that should allow the company to retain a good portion of its current user base without having to compete on price alone. Apple iOS users who purchase movies, TV shows, and applications from the iTunes store are unable to transmit these media to Android or other portable devices (while music is transferrable). iCloud adds another layer of switching costs by synchronizing media, photos, notes, and other items across all Apple devices. We believe an owner of an iOS device—say, an iPad—is less likely to switch from an iPhone to an Android phone if it means that the individual will be unable to sync or access a portion of his or her content. Additional Apple devices, such as the Mac and potentially an iWatch, could raise these switching costs even further.

BlackRock Asset managers such as BlackRock also benefit from switching costs. While the costs for investors might not be explicitly large, the perceived benefits of switching from one money manager to another are at times so uncertain that many investors take the path of least resistance and stay where they are. As a result, money that flows into asset-management firms tends to stay there—borne out by an average net annual redemption rate of only 30% for long-term mutual funds, which excludes the impact of money market funds, during the past 5-, 10-, 15-, 20-, and 25-year time frames. "Asset stickiness," or the degree to which money stays with an asset manager over time, plays a vital role in determining which companies in the asset management industry have the widest economic moats.

Looking more closely at BlackRock, which we feel has the widest moat in the asset management industry, we find that the company benefits from a diverse product portfolio, which is equally split among active and passive investment strategies. This effectively makes the firm agnostic to shifts among asset classes and investment strategies, limiting the impact that market swings can have on its overall level of managed assets. With much of BlackRock's AUM sourced from institutional clients, which tend to be more long-term-oriented than retail investors, the company has also been able to tap into a far stickier set of assets than many of its peers. While BlackRock may not be a household name, it is well known and well respected in the institutional channel, especially in fixed income, where it effectively forms an oligopoly with PIMCO and Legg Mason. BlackRock's ownership of iShares, the leading provider of exchange-traded funds, or ETFs, on a global basis, has endeared it to institutional investors, and should provide the firm with strong brand recognition in the retail advisor channel—in our view, the stickiest part of the retail channel. These attributes have all combined to build a wide economic moat around BlackRock's operations.

Rockwell Automation. Rockwell Automation has a wide economic moat thanks to a high degree of customer switching costs for its Logix automation control platform. Changing automation vendors is a decision not made lightly by a manufacturer; the organizational disruption caused by the change creates a number of potential costs for the customer, making sticking with the status quo the lower-friction choice. Think of the controller as the brains of the manufacturing floor. Any surgery involving it is delicate and approached with extreme care by the manufacturer. As a result, an automation firm such as Rockwell has a heavy incumbency advantage, building meaningful barriers to successful entry.

Network Effect

The network effect occurs when the value of a particular good or service increases for both new and existing users as more customers use that good or service. The network effect is a virtuous cycle that allows strong companies to become even stronger.

Key Questions: Network Effect

1. Explain how the value of the good or service increases as more customers and suppliers join the network. Try to provide quantitative proof that value (in real terms) increases faster than the rate of customer or supplier additions (with metrics like sales per user or sales per branch). With companies that truly benefit from the network effect, there's usually a clear, logical story for how value increases with additional customers and suppliers. Quantitative proof helps solidify the argument.

2. How does the company monetize its network? Many Internet companies have powerful network effects in the sense that the value of the service increases with additional users. Unfortunately, companies aren't always able to charge enough for the services they provide. Ability to sufficiently monetize the network through subscriptions, advertising, or charges provides a return to investors and ensures the company has money to reinvest in its network. Sufficient monetization of the network is a requirement for a narrow or wide moat.

3. Given that the offering's value increases as the network grows, do the company's suppliers and customers have strong bargaining power? How much value does the company have to share with its suppliers and customers? Sometimes suppliers or customers have bargaining power because the company needs them to increase the value of the network. If the company is in a weak bargaining position, it may be unable to sufficiently monetize its network.

Expedia and Priceline Major online travel agents, or OTAs, such as Expedia and Priceline are examples of companies whose economic profits are protected by the network effect. Both travel suppliers and consumers gravitate toward the big OTA platforms that consistently consolidate the largest collection of travel inventories and distribute them efficiently. Huge transaction volumes measured in billions of dollars each year run through the Expedia and Priceline families of booking sites. That's made these platforms a highly coveted distribution channel from the perspective of travel suppliers that are eager to list their services. In turn, this increases the appeal of the booking sites to travelers, thus setting off the virtuous cycle.

Tencent Tencent is among the most influential and profitable Internet firms in China, with a dominant position in instant messaging, online gaming, and social networking. By providing a high-quality online experience that has helped Chinese Internet users stay connected, informed, and entertained for more than a decade, Tencent has won the loyalty of several hundred million subscribers. Tracing its roots to an instant messaging service, Tencent has expanded into a massive and sticky online platform for 500 million Chinese Internet users during the past decade. Adding to its hugely popular QQ instant messaging service, which has more than 80% of share in terms of IM user time according to third-party researcher iResearch, Tencent has built its social networking and social media platforms to an impressive scale during the past few years. Tencent boasts more than 500 million accounts (though it's possible to have multiple accounts per user) both on the Qzone platform and on its Twitter-like microblog site, and it signed up more than 400 million users on mobile app WeChat, launched only two years ago. There are likely overlaps among the subscriber groups, but the numbers still serve to illustrate a network effect that Tencent's peers would be hard-pressed to match. Although Internet users can easily set up accounts on competing platforms, we think none of the rivals is close to the scale of Tencent. Leveraging its massive user base and site traffic, Tencent has been able to grab top shares in both online gaming and brand advertising despite being a late-comer to these markets.

Core Labs Core Labs provides the analytical firepower and tools needed to deeply study the geological structure and fluid dynamics of an oilfield reservoir. Core's efforts revolve around analyzing well cores and how hydrocarbons move through the reservoir, so it can suggest ways to improve recovery rates in a mature oilfield by a few hundred basis points. As compensation for its work, Core extracts just a fraction of its value to the operator through its fees, and the customer may be able to realize billions of dollars in incremental profits.

Core Labs is unique among its oil services peers thanks to its reservoir studies program. Companies pay a nominal fee to participate in an industry consortium—where more than 100 companies may participate—focused on how to best produce a certain reservoir. These studies are an important way for Core to strengthen relationships with a key group of customers while generating a significant network effect. By joining the studies, companies gain valuable knowledge relatively quickly and cheaply, while Core receives important data that the oil and gas firms have paid hundreds of millions, if not billions of dollars, to obtain. The network effect occurs because the more companies join the consortium, the more information Core can offer everyone, and the more value the offering has. Core's data analysis then provides the consortium with the needed information to properly allocate drilling capital. As reservoir dynamics change, the consortium studies naturally support further analysis of the reservoir and additional purchases of the associated services and equipment from Core. Oil and gas companies seeking the best techniques to exploit a given reservoir and thus generate the highest possible returns are compelled to take advantage of Core's position as a knowledge leader, by joining Core's studies and becoming regular users of Core's services.

Dassault Dassault Systèmes is a market-leading provider of 3-D computer-aided design, or CAD, and product lifecycle management, or PLM, software. Dassault's solutions allow its clients to design, collaborate, manufacture, and maintain products in a timely and cost-efficient manner. The company's flagship CAD product, SolidWorks, and leading PLM product, CATIA, are the driving forces behind the company's success (roughly 60% of group revenue), and a current roster of clients such as Boeing, BMW, Nokia, Nestle, and General Electric highlights the quality of the company's solutions. Dassault has an extensive education program that trains users from an early stage, high school and college, to be proficient in the company's tools, which creates a growing network of employees and employers that prefer Dassault products. This growing network of users provides the firm with a positive network effect, as students want to be trained on the software that most potential employers use, and employers want to use the software that most students know.

Efficient Scale

Efficient scale describes a dynamic in which a market of limited size is effectively served by one company or a small handful of companies. The incumbents generate economic profits, but a potential competitor is discouraged from entering because doing so would cause returns in the market to fall well below the cost of capital.

This phenomenon especially makes sense when a new entrant would have to sink a lot of capital. To cover its entry costs, it would want a sufficient share of the market, but if the market opportunity is limited, a fight for market share would cause prices to fall and hurt returns for all players in the industry. This barrier to entry relies on new entrants being rational. Knowing this, existing players often set prices that are high enough to generate sufficient returns on invested capital, but low enough to disincentivize prospective entrants.

Efficient scale differs from cost advantage, because the incumbent firm's cost advantage isn't necessarily difficult for a potential rival to replicate. It's just that the other potential players have no incentive to enter the market, even if they could ultimately achieve the same cost profile that incumbents have. Further, in cases where a specific or niche market is being served by a single firm, it doesn't make sense to say that the company has a low-cost advantage, because there's no basis for comparison.

Often, an efficient-scale business has a high degree of short- or medium-term pricing power. However, the company frequently chooses not to exercise this power to the fullest extent, even though doing so would maximize its current profitability. The business exercises restraint because it does not want to incent a rival to enter its market, which could destroy the economic rents for both players. The ability to exercise pricing power intelligently to influence the size of the "economic pie" in a way to both make sufficient profits and deter rivals is a distinguishing characteristic of efficient-scale businesses.

Key Questions: Efficient Scale

1. **Define the limits of the market. Is the addressable market finite or are the boundaries blurry? What is the size of the market, and what is the capacity of existing industry players? How many companies serve the industry?** Markets that lend themselves to the efficient-scale phenomenon are clearly defined and served by only a handful of players or fewer.

(Continued)

(Continued)
   2. **What is the cost of entering the market? How much market share would a new entrant have to grab in order to recoup the cost of entry?** These questions help assess the economics facing potential entrants.
   3. **Have potential competitors tried to enter the market and ultimately failed?** Evidence of failed entries can solidify an efficient-scale-based argument for a narrow or wide economic moat.

Pipelines Pipelines are arguably the best illustration of the efficient-scale classification, because these wide-moat companies don't benefit much from other sources of economic moat, yet they frequently demonstrate an ability to earn economic profits year after year. Suppose there's a need to move 250,000 barrels per day, or bpd, of crude oil from producing basin A to refining center B, and a pipeline exists that has the capacity to move 275,000 bpd along this route. There is no incentive for competitors to enter; the pipeline is efficiently scaled to the market. Pipelines have the added benefit of not needing to rely on potential entrants to be rational. The pipeline industry is heavily regulated because of environmental and safety concerns and eminent-domain considerations. In addition, regulators prevent the building of new pipelines unless there is a demonstrated economic need to do so. Because of the monopoly status of many pipelines, regulators also control rates but generally allow pipeline companies to earn an adequate return on their capital. This reflects the capital intensity of the business, as well as the regulated rates. However, remember that in our economic moat framework, it's the sustainability of excess economic profits that matters, not the size of the spread between ROIC and WACC. Because pipeline companies generally secure long-term contracts from their customers, and because there is little risk of technological disruption, these economic profits are very likely sustainable.

Mexican Airports Mexican airports provide another good example of companies that benefit from the efficient-scale phenomenon. These companies own the rights to operate geographic monopolies of airports in Mexico, allowing them to extract high economic profits from their customers. These monopolies resulted from the Mexican government's decision to privatize the country's main airports in 1998. As a result, Grupo Aeroportuario del Pacifico, Grupo Aeroportuario del Sureste, Grupo Aeroportuario del Centro Norte, and a privately owned firm were granted concessions to operate the airports for 50 years, significantly limiting competition. In return, the companies comply with the regulation of fees charged to airlines and passengers and make necessary infrastructure investments. To comply with the granted concessions, the private airport operators must submit a master development program, or MDP, every five years to the Ministry of Communication and Transportation for review and approval. The MDP contains proposed capital spending on each airport for the next five-year and subsequent 10-year periods. The Ministry then uses the MDP and other factors to arrive at the maximum rate that operators will be allowed to charge departing passengers. Beyond the intangible asset of the government concession, Mexican airports benefit from the efficient-scale phenomenon because many cities can support only one major airport.

Notes

1. At Morningstar, we calculate ROIC as earnings before interest (EBI) divided by invested capital, where EBI is operating income (excluding charges) plus amortization less cash taxes and invested capital is operating assets less operating liabilities. WACC is defined as (cost of debt) × (weight of debt) + (cost of equity) × (weight of equity).

3

Why Moat Trends Matter

Contributed by Stephen Ellis, a member of Morningstar's Economic Moat Committee and head of Financial Services equity research at Morningstar

By now you have a good working knowledge of economic moats and what it takes for companies to build them. But there's another important facet of moats that we haven't much touched on—the direction they're heading. Moat ratings, while forward looking, are static, and don't indicate whether a company's competitive position is improving or declining. That's why in 2009, we introduced moat trend ratings to supplement our economic moat ratings. The trend ratings convey the direction firms are heading, in terms of their competitive advantages. We believe this is a very important additional piece of information. Moat ratings can tell you the width of a company's current moat, but trend ratings tell you if that moat is holding up well, is getting even stronger, or is in danger of being filled in by a rampaging horde of invaders.

Trend ratings recognize that corporations evolve and that moats grow, mature, and eventually die. In other words, economic moats have a life cycle. As such, whenever we assign a moat rating, we also assign a trend rating: positive when competitive advantages are improving, negative when they're declining, and stable when we don't see much movement one way or the other. In mid-2013, about 16% of the companies we cover had negative trends, while just 8% showed positive trends. This means that positive trend ratings are even rarer than our hard-to-attain wide moat ratings, which we've awarded to about 13% of our coverage universe.

Given that our time horizon when assessing moats is 10 to 20 years, focusing more attention on how the competitive environment is currently changing is a useful enhancement to our overall moat methodology. We want to minimize situations where we've mischaracterized a competitive threat as not serious, only to find the need to downgrade a firm's moat after it has been overtaken by attackers. As analysts and investors, we're now explicitly charged with assessing the expected future changes in a firm's competitive advantages, and separating competitive threats that are merely temporary in nature from more dangerous and permanent changes in the overall environment. In short, we think adding moat trends to our toolbox can provide a more complete picture of a firm's competitiveness.

Figure 3.1 shows how positive and negative moat trends are distributed across Morningstar's current coverage universe by sector.

When evaluating moat trends, we start by looking at the same five sources of moat that we use when determining moat ratings (intangible assets, cost advantage, switching costs, network effect, and efficient scale). For example, if a company's moat is based on a low-cost base of manufacturing plants

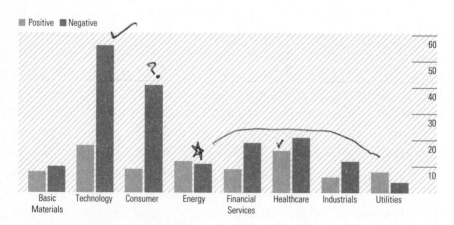

Figure 3.1  Moat Trends by Sector (%)
SOURCE: Morningstar Equity Research.

and it's expanding its capacity, we want to know if it's widening the cost gap between itself and its competitors. Or perhaps a company with an existing low-cost advantage is in the midst of developing network effect as an additional moat source. Factors like these strengthen the case for a positive moat trend rating.

Moat Trends and Fundamental Performance

When we look at data extracted from our analysts' discounted cash flow models for positive- and negative-trend companies, in Table 3.1, we find that positive-trend firms tend to grow more quickly, produce more profits, and

Table 3.1   Median Metrics: Growth, Profitability, Valuation

	S&P 500 (%)	Positive Trends (%)	Negative Trends (%)
Trailing 3-Year EPS CAGR	11.9	14.7	2.1
Projected 5-Year EPS CAGR	9.4	13.6	7.3
Trailing 3-Year Revenue Growth	7.9	12.8	4.8
Projected 5-Year Revenue Growth	5.2	9.2	3.8
Projected 5-Year EBIT Growth	7.8	12.7	6.8
Trailing 3-Year Operating Margin	15.7	15.9	11.9
Projected 5-Year Operating Margin	17.4	19.4	13.2
Trailing 3-Year Average ROIC	13.0	10.9	11.4
Projected 5-Year Average ROIC	12.6	12.4	9.8
Forward Debt/ EBITDA	1.72	1.5	1.45
Forward EBITDA/ Interest Expense	11.7	11.8	8.4
Forward P/E	16.0	17.8	13.8

Source: Morningstar Equity Research.

generate higher returns on invested capital than firms included in the S&P 500. On the other hand, negative-trend firms generally show weaker metrics than both positive-trend firms and the S&P 500 firms. This makes sense, given our focus on competitive advantages. The weaker firms are usually losing market share, unable to raise prices to offset their costs, or being undercut by competitors. In contrast, the positive-trend firms tend to show stronger metrics because their improving competitive picture—perhaps including market-share gains or increased economies of scale—is leading to higher growth rates and improved profitability.

Five Key Considerations for Moat Trends

It is possible to have a wide economic moat rating and a positive trend, as well as a no-moat rating and a negative trend.

Companies with no-moat and negative trend ratings aren't necessarily in imminent danger of bankruptcy, but we do believe these firms' strategic and competitive positions are already weak and becoming worse over time. We also see wide-moat companies with positive trends that are still strengthening their moats. A wide-moat company already has great competitive advantages, and if these advantages are becoming even stronger or if the company is developing additional moat sources, we may award it a positive moat rating.

Moat and trend ratings are independent.

We evaluate moat and trend ratings independently. We view the trend rating as an indicator of how the firm's competitive advantages are evolving within its given moat band. For example, a positive trend rating on a narrow-moat company indicates that the company's competitive advantages are improving, but the qualitative and quantitative characteristics of the firm's moat might not be strong enough to warrant a wide moat. Also, when a moat rating changes, we still evaluate the trend rating separately. For instance, if we have a narrow-moat company with a negative trend, we could decide to downgrade it to no moat but the trend could remain negative.

As you can see in Figure 3.2, while we view economic moat ratings on a three-part spectrum, there are gradients within each bucket. Some wide-moat companies have stronger, more durable competitive advantages than other

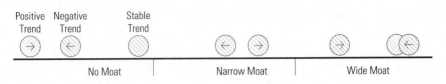

Figure 3.2   Independence of Economic Moat and Moat Trend Ratings
SOURCE: Morningstar Equity Research.

wide-moat companies. You could say that these wide-moat companies are at the widest end of the wide category, and on the spectrum below, a stronger wide-moat company would sit to the right of a weaker wide-moat company. However, we don't use the trend rating to indicate a company's position on the spectrum below. The stronger, wider-moat company may have a negative trend rating, while the weaker wide-moat company may have a positive trend rating. Each company is starting from a different position of strength, and the competitive advantages are heading in different directions.

Changes in ROIC do not necessarily affect our evaluation of moat trends.

Although rising ROICs are often associated with positive moat trends, this certainly doesn't have to be the case. ROICs can go up for many non-moat-related reasons. For example, product cycles and cyclicality will have a major effect on ROICs. Business mix changes may also alter ROICs without changing the moat dynamic. It's even possible to have a negative moat trend and rising ROICs, for a while at least. For example, if a business without many growth prospects stops or slows down its investments (thereby "harvesting" its moat), it may very well experience rising returns for a number of years as its invested capital base declines in relation to profitability and asset turnover.

By the same token, falling ROICs aren't automatically a sign that the trend is negative. ROICs can decline for a number of reasons—some of them actually good. When a firm makes a significant investment that will ultimately strengthen its economic moat, ROICs may decline. Perhaps it's spending heavily on advertising or R&D to strengthen its intangible assets, or it might be building a major new factory that will eventually lower its costs. In both cases, the project is not generating earnings today, which depresses ROICs, but the firm is making the right long-term moves to sustain its competitive advantages. Thinking about moat trends extends beyond ROICs.

Moat trends are not necessarily related to growth.

High revenue growth or a sharp decline in revenue doesn't indicate whether a firm has a positive or negative trend. Perhaps a company's revenue is on the rise because it's operating in a very high-growth market, but competition is intense and there are very few barriers to entry, threatening its ability to continue growing. Alternatively, revenue could temporarily decline if a business is undergoing a cyclical downturn, or if a customer delays an order of new components. It's important to look at how the firm's moat sources are changing over time rather than simple revenue growth to properly assess its competitive position.

Business-mix shift does not affect our trend ratings.

There are two schools of thought around how to take shifts in a company's business mix into consideration when evaluating moat trends. The first maintains that a company with a business mix that is shifting toward moatier segments over time deserves a positive trend. The second holds that business mix doesn't have an effect on the trend rating (though it is still important for determining economic moat ratings) because a shifting business mix merely indicates the presence of a higher-growth segment with a moat, rather than actual improvements or deteriorations in competitive positioning for the separate businesses on a stand-alone basis. We believe the second approach is more valid because it focuses attention on how the firm's competitive advantages are changing rather than on simple growth rates. It's consistent with our overall methodology, which emphasizes moats, to put a greater emphasis on improving or deteriorating competitive advantages rather than simple growth or decline. In addition, if we see a management team making poor capital-allocation decisions—perhaps acquiring a large company that doesn't have a moat, thereby "diworsifying" its previously wide-moat business—we can downgrade the moat to narrow, given the new business mix, or a give the company a Poor stewardship rating. (See the next chapter for more on our stewardship ratings. We find that management's capital-allocation decisions can have such a big impact on a company's competitive positioning and economic profit potential that assessing the leadership team's stewardship of shareholder capital is an important aspect of our research process.)

Probably the best way to learn how to evaluate moat trend is to look at some real-life scenarios and see how we've analyzed various situations and determined moat trends. Because the starting point for evaluating any moat trend should be determining which moat source is affected, we've grouped these case studies by moat source.

Intangibles

Intangible moat sources include patents, brands, research and development strength, and regulatory environment, as well as other items that are, by definition, hard to quantify. Moats based around intangibles are common within the healthcare sector because of its reliance on patents, but the industry is currently a bit split in terms of positive and negative trends. On the one hand, you have a firm like pharmaceutical giant AstraZeneca, which has suffered through a long period of declining R&D productivity that began in the 2000s after the industry experienced a surge of innovation in the 1980s and 1990s. Simply put, AstraZeneca is struggling to develop new and innovative drugs to replace its drugs coming off patent, while the FDA is being more careful about which drugs it approves, making it even harder for AstraZeneca to replace declining drugs with newer ones.

But while big pharma has struggled with R&D productivity over the past decade, biotechnology firms have been remarkably productive, and many of them enjoy positive moat trends today. A key common factor for these positive trends is a proprietary R&D platform, which allows biotech firms such as Regeneron and Seattle Genetics to screen for and select molecules or antibodies that have a higher chance of being successful. In other words, there's knowledge sharing going on at each of these companies, which makes them far more productive than their peers from a research and technology perspective and gives them positive trend ratings.

These biotechs are each leveraging a single development platform into multiple solutions, and with each additional application found, we think the intangible moat source strengthens. For example, Seattle Genetics has developed an antibody-drug conjugate, or ADC, technology platform. With ADCs, antibodies are directly linked to potent chemotherapeutics, making treatment more targeted and effective. The antibodies themselves (such as Herceptin for breast cancer), which already have substantial killing power, can bind to a cancer cell and effectively transport cancer chemotherapeutics into the cancer cell where its payload is released. The end result is that nasty side effects are less common, as the antibody sticks to the cancer cells and more of the cancer drug is delivered to the sick cells. These ADCs have been described as floating sea mines or miniature drug bombs. Today, Seattle Genetics has one of the more powerful technology platforms for screening and selecting the most effective floating linkers (or mines) for its own drugs, and its linkers are commonly used for next-generation cancer drugs developed through partner collaborations. In short, as the firm's experience with its platform increases, its linkers become part of more drugs and the company improves its ability to charge higher royalties to its partners. Given these factors, we think Seattle Genetics' intangibles-based moat should continue to widen. Figure 3.3 shows its position in antibody drug conjugates, relative to its peers.

Procter & Gamble, by contrast, is an illuminating case study on how even some of the most powerful brands on the planet can lose cachet in the eyes of consumers. Over the past decade, P&G's ability to innovate has slowed, while its competitors have rapidly closed the gap. In an industry where a single point of market share is a huge deal, P&G has struggled across several markets. For example, Gillette has lost share in the razor and blades market since 2005, and P&G's beauty care brands, Pantene and Olay, have also struggled. Perhaps the most high-profile example of P&G's challenges is in the laundry area. P&G

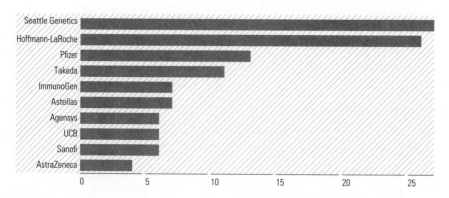

Figure 3.3   Top 10 Sponsors of Ongoing Clinical Trials of Antibody Drug Conjugates
Data as of October 2012.
Source: TrialTrove.

lost roughly 70 basis points of value share in the liquid laundry detergent market between 2007 and 2012 in North America, while its domestic unit share declined to less than 56% by the end of calendar year 2012. P&G was forced to reduce prices to regain share, and the timely introduction of the Tide Pods in early 2012 after eight years of research also helped it garner a larger share of the overall market. Tide Pods are now a $500 million business in the $7.5 billion U.S. liquid laundry detergent category.

Despite the Pods' success, we still think P&G faces a negative trend for several reasons. First, the company is no longer outspending peers in terms of research investment as a percentage of sales. As a result, the Tide Pods are P&G's first new major innovation in more than a decade. Second, when CEO A.G. Lafley took over P&G in 2000, he decentralized R&D efforts, tying results more closely to short-term profit goals. As a result, new product introductions in the 2000s were cut in half as the research focus shifted toward reformulating existing products versus delivering category game-changers. Former CEO Bob McDonald had worked to centralize research efforts, but he was too aggressive in chasing emerging markets while intense competition in North America hurt the firm, particularly as consumers in the wake of the Great Recession became more value conscious and less enamored by P&G's often premium-priced products. Now, with McDonald ousted, the firm is back under CEO Lafley's hand, and with P&G's earlier announcement of a $10 billion spending reduction plan, we worry again that the firm could cut R&D and ultimately innovation, to P&G's long-term competitive detriment. Third, we believe the competitive environment has simply grown far more intense over the past decade, and it will continue to do so going forward. For example, Unilever can easily roll out products in 60 countries today in the same time it once took to launch a product in 10 countries, which is an ability that once belonged to P&G alone. Even within the pod laundry category, we note that a 72-count package of Tide Pods at Wal-Mart is priced at an 80% premium versus the same-size package of Pods by All (owned by Germany's Henkel) and more than double the cost of Purex UltraPacks (owned by Sun Products). The fact that two major competitors were able to launch competing pod products so quickly despite eight years of work by P&G is troubling and speaks to the limited and shrinking R&D advantage P&G has over its peers, as illustrated by Figure 3.4. For all of these reasons, we believe P&G's ability to charge premium prices will continue to erode going forward if consumers don't perceive the value differential as compelling.

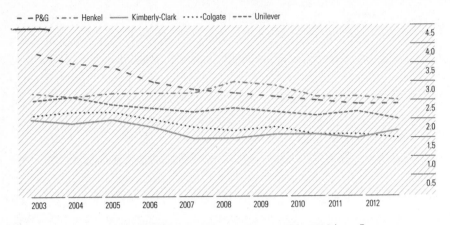

Figure 3.4   Procter & Gamble R&D Spending vs. Peers, 2003–2012 (as a Percentage of Revenue)
SOURCE: Company reports.

Cost Advantage

Everyone knows the package-shipping duo of UPS and FedEx. Both firms enjoy massive scale advantages thanks to large transportation networks of aircraft and trucks, distribution hubs, and the use of technology to deliver millions of packages on time to businesses and consumers around the world every day. The cost for effectively competing with these giants in the domestic U.S. market, where they still derive more than 75% of sales, can be measured in the billions. Just ask rival DHL, which lost nearly $10 billion over a fruitless decade as it tried and failed to compete in the U.S. market in the 2000s before retreating. Meanwhile, FedEx has been gaining market share over UPS in U.S. ground operations for more than a decade, as Figure 3.5 shows, earning it a positive moat trend.

What's the secret behind FedEx's success? Up until the late 1990s, FedEx generally controlled the airborne market while UPS controlled the ground delivery market. In fact, FedEx thought so little of the ground market in the mid-1990s that it viewed "trucks" as a four-letter word. This situation changed in the late 1990s as UPS targeted FedEx's airborne market and became the shipper of choice for Internet giants such as eBay and Amazon. The airborne market was also in the early stages of a secular shift, as cost-conscious companies have traded down to cheaper ground delivery options over the past decade, causing the airborne market to shrink. FedEx realized it had to effectively

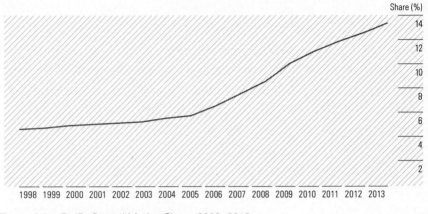

Share (%)

1998 1999 2000 2001 2002 2003 2004 2005 2006 2007 2008 2009 2010 2011 2012 2013

Figure 3.5   , 2002–2013
SOURCE: FedEx, Morningstar estimates.

counter UPS and invade the U.S ground space, so FedEx Ground was borne out of the rebranding of Roadway Package System, or RPS, a Pittsburgh-based firm that FedEx acquired in 1998 and UPS' biggest ground rival at the time.

FedEx's primary advantage in this fight has been its cost structure. UPS relies on an army of brown-uniform-clad union employees, while FedEx relies on nonemployee independent contractors for both pickup and delivery, and line-haul truck driving. FedEx's drivers are motivated by a pay system that rewards higher volume and on-time deliveries, while also encouraging employees to feel like entrepreneurs. Drivers are paid based on the number of stops they make, the number of packages they handle, and the density of the delivery zones. Complaints and missed deliveries jeopardize driver bonuses. In contrast, UPS' unionized workers are certainly loyal, but they're not quite as motivated to drive sales as FedEx's employees are.

FedEx's second advantage is technology. In early 2013, FedEx could deliver ground packages faster than UPS on almost a third of its routes, at equal speed to UPS on two thirds of its routes, and slower than UPS on just 3% of the routes. This comparison owes partly to FedEx's distribution hubs, which are highly automated, with human hands touching the package only when it's unloaded from the trailer and loaded into another truck after being sorted. The actual sorting process—which includes capturing a package's physical dimensions, weight, destination zip code, and where it is in the process at any given moment—is completely automated and measured in milliseconds. FedEx has also forced its sorting-equipment vendors into using FedEx's own custom sorting and packaging software solution, rather than relying on the equipment vendor's software solution, similar to the way Wal-Mart has forced suppliers to meet its own shipping specifications rather than set their own. Given FedEx's increased control over the sorting process, it typically re-engineers its delivery lanes twice a year, seeking to speed up delivery times to more than 80,000 zip codes.

FedEx's workforce structure and speed advantages are very profitable. FedEx Ground is far more profitable than FedEx's airborne unit, thanks to the cheaper cost of running trucks versus airplanes. Operating margins hit nearly 20% for FedEx Ground in early 2013, versus just 6% for airborne. Given FedEx's continued market-share gains and still-growing cost and technology advantages, we think FedEx is a great example of a positive trend based on cost advantages.

For an example of a negative moat trend, look to major oil companies such as ExxonMobil, Chevron, and Total, which are all seeing declining competitive advantages due to a weakening cost structure. We've long said that the era of cheap oil is over, and these companies are the ones primarily affected by that shift. The easiest way to describe this shift is to consider that in 2008, conventional oil and natural gas production made up 77% of the total production of the large-market-cap oil producers that we covered. By 2016, we estimate that conventional production will make up only 62% of total oil and gas output. What will make up the gap? More expensive deep-water oil, liquefied natural gas, or LNG, and tight oil and gas production. All in all, we expect capital spending per barrel to increase 30% to $41 per barrel of oil equivalent, up from $32 in 2008. Here's another way of looking at the problem: As Figure 3.6 shows, the majors spent $120 billion in 2012 on oil and gas projects versus around $40 billion in 2001, yet they produced less as a group in 2012 than they did in 2001. That's an expensive proposition for shareholders!

Beyond the shifting cost dynamics, the major oil companies' advantages just aren't what they were in the 1960s, when the industry consisted of the Seven Sisters controlling 85% of the world's reserves. Today, those super-majors control just 6% of the world's oil and gas reserves, while OPEC and the state-owned national oil companies control nearly 90%. The shift in reserves ownership, combined with the increase in oil prices over the past decade, has meant that the national oil companies have increasingly enjoyed substantial bargaining power. In the past, the majors could provide both technical expertise and capital to the national oil companies, who were starved of both in a low oil price environment. That's not the case today. With oil selling for about $100 per

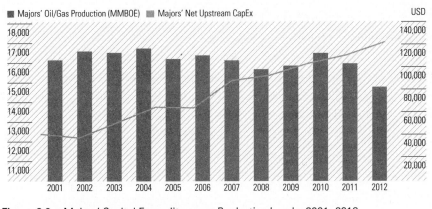

Figure 3.6 Majors' Capital Expenditures vs. Production Levels, 2001–2012
Note: Ten-year production CAGR: 0.5%. Ten-year CapEx CAGR: 12%.
Source: Morningstar estimates, company reports.

barrel, Saudi Arabia enjoys foreign exchange reserves worth more than $700 billion, and Saudi Aramco (the country's national oil company) plans to spend more than $200 billion in the next decade on oil and gas projects and investment in oilfield technology such as nanotechnology. The cash windfall has also allowed national oil companies to pursue assets outside of their own borders, competing with the majors in many cases, but also demanding better contract terms. The shift in bargaining power means countries with reserves can demand and obtain contracts with the oil and gas majors that essentially let the countries claim 99% of the revenues generated from the agreement over time, as with Iraq. The best avenues left for growth for the Western majors and international oil companies are areas that the national oil companies do not control, such as deep-water oil in the Gulf of Mexico, Australian LNG, and the Canadian oil sands, where obtaining oil costs far more than the $10 a barrel it costs to do so in Saudi Arabia. As a result of all of these factors, we believe the major oil companies' competitive advantages are declining and their moat trends are negative.

Switching Costs

The tech sector is particularly challenging territory for evaluating moats and trends, but it also offers some of the clearest examples of the power of switching costs. For corporations, switching among different software providers can be immensely expensive, especially if the software becomes part of the key operating practices of the business. Moreover, IT departments are often resistant to change because they don't want the hassle of learning new software, building new customizations, and training new users. Switching to an alternative software program can also lead to lost productivity and security issues, and if a rollout doesn't go as planned, the switch can be scrapped at a cost of millions of dollars. Thanks to these high switching costs, good business-oriented software companies can be viewed almost like annuities that generate a constant stream of cash every year through license renewals with relatively little technology risk.

One of our favorite companies within this space is Cerner, which provides electronic medical systems for hospitals, pharmacies, and stand-alone medical practices. Cerner offers a complete technology architecture for a hospital, allowing doctors, nurses, laboratory technicians, pharmacists, and other healthcare professionals to provide a better and more efficient experience, while lowering the odds of mistakes. One of the key benefits of using Cerner's systems is the ability for doctors to review and update a patient's healthcare record from any facility, which is particularly useful when a patient ends up going to multiple offices for care and keeping up-to-date records is difficult. Doctors can also place orders for prescriptions, manage schedules, order tests, provide the required information for patient transfers (a source of many errors), and provide patients with timely electronic access to test results. Billing is also more straightforward, as everything is captured electronically, reducing the odds of data entry errors. Once a system is implemented, the switching costs are immense. Cerner deals with life-and-death situations in many cases, and disrupting workflows for a software change is simply not an option, as its 99% renewal rates can attest.

The electronic healthcare systems industry is still in its infancy, and we see Cerner's switching costs only increasing from here. The 2009 Health Information Technology for Economic and Clinical Health Act, or HITECH, is not only providing substantial monetary incentives (more than $35 billion) to doctors to adopt electronic healthcare records, or EHR, it also requires doctors to demonstrate meaningful use of the system by actually integrating it deeply within their current daily workflows. Regulation is literally entrenching Cerner and its peers! After 2015, physicians not using EHR will be penalized 1% of Medicare payments, and the penalty will gradually increase over time.

The HITECH Act by itself is not enough to convince us that Cerner's competitive advantages are improving, because the act serves an industry tailwind propelling many companies. However, meeting the meaningful-use requirements to earn the incentive payments is challenging for these firms. Currently, there are three separate stages of meaningful use, and the first two stages include around 50 requirements that must be met. Meeting these requirements requires a tightly integrated system because information has to be transmitted between pharmacists, doctors, nurses, insurance agencies, public health organizations, and immunization registries along with other parties in a fairly seamless manner. Today, different systems are often used by doctors, nurses, and others to manage information, and Cerner's competitors have only worsened the problem. Cerner competitors such as Allscripts, McKesson, and MEDITECH have acquired various systems and technologies over the past few years, and as a result, their overall systems are a blend of different types of software rather than a smoothly integrated solution developed from the ground up (Cerner, by contrast, uses its own clinical programming language called Synapse). The growth-by-acquisition strategy has caused delays when rolling out systems for hospitals, causing these competitors to miss deadlines for meaningful-use incentive payments. As a result, Cerner's organically built system is increasingly taking market share away from these legacy providers, as it can more easily meet meaningful-use deadlines.

We see the meaningful-use guidelines as especially important to Cerner because they are forcing medical professionals to develop new habits based on Cerner's system, and once developed, these habits are hard to break. Forming new habits around e-prescriptions, test ordering, and billing practices really just scratches the surface of Cerner's growing switching costs. Cerner also offers population management tools that enable doctors to track all of their patients with a specific condition, see their tests results, and track how their therapy is progressing. Cerner's software algorithms can analyze a patient's healthcare record (think of trying to sort through a huge binder stuffed with information in a minute or two) and identify the most important information for professionals within seconds. These types of innovations encourage healthcare professionals to rely on Cerner as an analytical tool rather than as a simple transaction and record-keeping system. We think these factors create a virtuous cycle for Cerner and a positive moat trend.

Despite our fondness for software-based moats, these moats can and do erode over time. A case in point is SAP. SAP's strength is enterprise resource planning, or ERP, software, which helps corporations manage marketing, sales and distribution, production planning, assets accounting, supply chain management, cost control, project management, plant maintenance, and human resources all within a single software package. Beyond the substantial annual licensing fees that SAP charges, just implementing SAP's software can cost tens of millions of dollars, involve extensive training of the workforce, and require outside consultants to oversee the implementation process. Companies also need to hire dedicated IT professionals to manage the overall platform, including the needed servers and disk drives. Even then, things can go wrong and the company's core processes can be bungled, which not only angers current customers but can also cost tens of millions of dollars more in lost sales. Given the immense costs and efforts involved, SAP users do tend to be very sticky.

However, with the rise of cloud-based and software-as-a-service, or SaaS, computing, those switching costs are in decline. Popularized by Salesforce.com, software-as-a-service offers a very different model for customers and is highly disruptive to SAP's business. Salesforce.com's revenue increased 48% annually between 2004 and 2012. SAP's software is called *on-premise* because the key data resides on customers' servers, but SaaS turns that premise on its head. Salesforce.com's offering is hosted entirely on the web, on Salesforce.com servers, which requires only an Internet browser to use—dedicated IT professionals and consultants aren't needed. This SaaS option can create significant savings for companies, as Figure 3.7 shows.

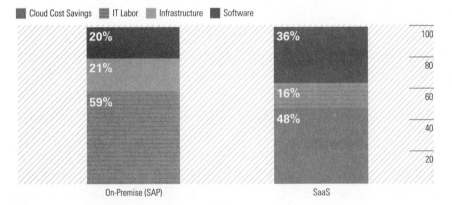

Figure 3.7   Five-Year Total Cost of Ownership (%)
Source: Salesforce.com, IDC.

SaaS shifts software to a variable-cost model based on usage and changing corporate needs, versus a fixed annual license fee. Salesforce.com and its peers have seen success primarily with customer relationship management, or CRM, applications recently, but new SaaS modules are also on the market for human resources, accounting, and supply chain planning, among other uses. In other words, over time the entire enterprise resource-planning software will be available through the cloud and likely through a single vendor. Given the ease of installation, the conversion of a fixed cost into a variable cost, and the much lower operating expenses due to not needing IT professionals, we see SAP's ERP on-premise software gradually being displaced within corporations by the more flexible SaaS solution. It remains to be seen if SAP can successfully reinvent itself by offering SaaS versions of its legacy on-premise applications.

Network Effect

The network effect, in our view, is one of the most powerful moat sources a company can have. This is the primary force behind the economic moats for U.S. e-commerce powerhouses Amazon and eBay. Basically, a marketplace becomes more valuable as it increases in size because the value of the services provided increases as the user base expands. Facebook, with its one billion-plus monthly users, is another great example of the network effect in action.

MercadoLibre is one of the most intriguing examples of a positive trend due to the network effect. MercadoLibre (translated to "free market" in English) is the dominant e-commerce player in Latin America and offers an online marketplace very similar to eBay's and Amazon's marketplaces. Since 1999, the firm has expanded country-by-country in South America, successfully growing in fragmented markets with individual transportation, customs, and regulatory barriers to entry versus the relatively homogeneous U.S. market. Unlike in the U.S., where Internet penetration is around 80% (and among those users, broadband penetration is close to 90%), total Internet penetration within Latin America is less than 50%, with broadband penetration in the single-digit range. As you might expect, these numbers are increasing rapidly, with both e-commerce sales and Internet user adoption growing at double-digit rates. MercadoLibre's base of 90 million users will surely grow, as 100 million new Internet users are expected in the region over the next few years. More importantly, because MercadoLibre's user base is already so large, new entrants face nearly insurmountable barriers to entry to duplicate its marketplace's value to users, which means MercadoLibre's network is very likely to capture greater than its fair share of the new users coming online.

What makes MercadoLibre's network-effect advantage even more compelling and durable is its rather interesting strategy. The firm makes no secret of the fact that it has copied many of the elements that have made Amazon, eBay (which owns an 18% stake in MercadoLibre), and PayPal so successful. You may have heard the saying that "good artists copy, great artists steal," and that's applicable here. For example, MercadoLibre has focused primarily on fixed-price listings, avoiding the "auction bubble" and sometimes painful transition that eBay has endured in recent years as it's moved its business toward more fixed-price listings. MercadoLibre also has a very simple fee structure with a single final value fee of about 6.5% versus the multiple fees that eBay charges, which is an ongoing source of frustration for eBay sellers. What's more, MercadoLibre's already-low fees compared with its peers leave little room for competitors to attack by undercutting on fees. The firm is borrowing ideas from other firms as well. It's offering a PayPal clone through its MercadoPago, which is generating around $2 billion in annual payment volumes (PayPal is well over $100 billion). It's also taking ideas from craigslist with a growing classified business, and from Google by offering ads on its pages. Figure 3.8 gives a look at MercadoLibre's growing user base and MercadoPago's increasing payment volumes.

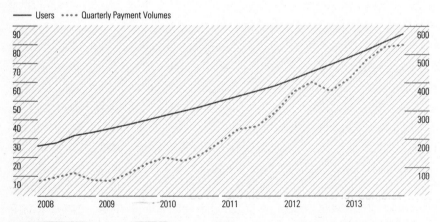

Figure 3.8   Growth in MercadoLibre's User Base and MercadoPago Payment Volumes (in Millions)
Source: MercadoLibre.

To see the network effect working in reverse, look at the Nasdaq, which has a negative trend rating, and the New York Stock Exchange, which had a negative trend rating when it was a stand-alone company before being acquired by IntercontinentalExchange Group in late 2013. In the past, each exchange benefited from being the major source of liquidity for investors wishing to trade, and the brand cachet associated with being on the NYSE in particular attracted many high-quality companies. For the NYSE, it was a great business model for more than 200 years, until it wasn't. In the late 1990s and early 2000s, a combination of improving technology and evolving regulation led to increased competition for stock trading.

In retrospect, the industry's increasing emphasis on speed, technology, and low transaction costs signaled the decline of the exchanges' competitive advantages. Electronic trading gave rise to high-frequency trading shops that can move in and out of trades within milliseconds for a fraction of a cent per share in profit. These companies make up anywhere from 50% to 75% of daily trading activity today on the exchanges, and their primary concern is the processing speed and cost of their trades, not any brand cachet associated with trading on the NYSE or Nasdaq. As a result, the Nasdaq and NYSE were outgunned by technology-savvy entrants such as Direct Edge and BATS, which were able to take advantage of increases in computing power to offer faster and better executions, with trade execution times now measured in milliseconds. In addition, the new entrants were largely owned by the Wall Street banks such as J.P. Morgan, which wanted to offer private pools of liquidity to clients.

The market's shifting needs and priorities meant that the original exchanges were constantly forced into cutting prices and offering rebates to customers to maintain liquidity, but to no avail. NYSE and Nasdaq were no longer the primary avenues for buying and selling shares (which, unlike more protected products such as futures, are fungible), but rather each became just one of many providers, negating the value of their network-based moats. As a result, in 2006, the NYSE's market share for transactions on its listed stocks dipped below 75% for the first time since 1976. The declines have continued since then, and in mid-2013, the NYSE matched only about 32% of the transaction volumes for stocks listed on the NYSE. The Nasdaq has seen a similar decline in its market share, and its matched share of Nasdaq-listed company volume stands at 30% in 2013, down from 52% in 2006, as illustrated by Figure 3.9. While the rate of market-share losses has slowed recently as the

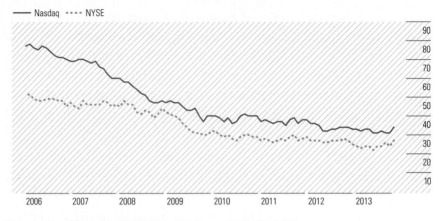

Figure 3.9   Nasdaq and NYSE Market Share, 2006–2013 (%)
Source: Nasdaq, NYSE.

exchanges have battled back with new and faster trading systems, we don't expect the competitive environment to improve. Traders will likely shift order flow between electronic networks (both public and privately owned dark pools, which offer institutional investors nonexchange sources of liquidity where trades are concealed from the public) to obtain the best execution and prices, putting constant pricing pressure on the exchanges to cut prices to maintain enough liquidity.

Efficient Scale

Our newest moat source, efficient scale, was introduced only in late 2011. Recall that efficient scale refers to situations where companies are effectively serving a very limited market size, and potential competitors have little incentive to enter the market because by doing so, they would lower the industry's returns to below the cost of capital. Although this moat source hasn't been part of our framework for long, we have identified several situations where we believe the efficient-scale advantage for a firm is changing in positive or negative way.

For example, there's an entire category of biotechnology firms focused on orphan drugs that derive their moats from efficient scale. Congress passed the Orphan Drug Act of 1983 to promote the development of drugs that treat rare diseases, where the patient population might only be in the hundreds or thousands globally versus the millions that are treated for, say, high cholesterol. The issue was that drug companies, in response to earlier legislation (the Kefauver Harris Amendment in the early 1960s), were focusing only on developing drugs that could treat large populations and common diseases; that was the most effective way to recover the large costs of moving drugs through expensive clinical trials to meet the U.S. Food and Drug Administration's tough safety and effectiveness requirements. By the early 1980s, many conditions were said to be *orphaned*, with no treatments available because the pharmaceutical companies deemed it uneconomical to develop them. In short, the small patient population couldn't possibly pay enough for the drugs for the companies to recover their development expenses.

The Orphan Drug Act essentially meant that drug companies would be granted lucrative regulatory benefits in exchange for developing drugs for orphaned diseases, making it economically feasible to pursue these patient populations. Drugs currently qualify for orphan status if the U.S. patient population is fewer than 200,000 patients. Benefits for drug companies include a seven-year period of market exclusivity, tax incentives, grants for drug development, and fast-track approvals. The legislation is widely believed to be a success, with more than 1,000 drugs granted orphan status in the past few decades, versus just 38 drugs prior to the act being passed.

From a moat-focused perspective, orphan drugs are very attractive, as the markets are typically best served by just a single firm. Morningstar covers several orphan-drug companies, including Alexion and BioMarin Pharmaceutical, both of which have narrow moats. It's not hard to see why. Alexion's Soliris is the only drug approved to treat paroxysmal nocturnal hemoglobinuria, a disease that destroys red blood cells and causes anemia, fatigue, and blood clots, killing half of its sufferers within 15 years. In addition to developing the drug, Alexion has worked hard to identify and reach out to a population of just 8,000 to 10,000 patients and educate doctors about the treatment. For its efforts, Alexion is charging $400,000 to $500,000 per year for Soliris. BioMarin has a portfolio of drugs for various diseases, including Aldurazyme, which treats mucopolysaccharidosis I, or MPS I. MPS I sufferers do not produce enough of one of the 11 enzymes required to break down sugar chains into molecules, and suffer from bone, organ, and brain damage as a result. Again, only about 3,000 people suffer from this disease, and BioMarin charges $200,000 annually for the drug, making it about a $200 million product line. In addition to the exclusivity period granted by the Orphan Drug Act, these drugs tend to be very difficult to manufacture, making it even less likely that a new entrant will want to pursue these small markets.

What makes these firms even more attractive is their ability to expand their rare drugs to new markets, thus creating positive moat trends. Because an efficient-scale market is one that can be effectively served by a single firm, a positive trend can occur when a company can expand a drug's indications to serve multiple rare-disease niches and thus numerous efficient-scale markets. Alexion is pursuing this course with Soliris, testing it for several additional diseases such as severe and relapsing neuromyelitis optica (which causes eye pain, vision loss, limb weakness or paralysis, and loss of bladder and bowel control), Shiga-toxin-production E. coli hemolytic uremic syndrome (which causes organ damage), and severe and refractory myasthenia gravis (which causes blurred vision, slurred speech, and difficulty chewing, swallowing, and breathing). Given the very limited number of competitors Soliris will face in each rare market, we see the firm as expanding its competitive advantages with each new indication. BioMarin also exhibits its positive trend as it expands its rare-disease portfolio with new drugs and new indications in the coming few years. As an added bonus for orphan-focused firms, the FDA is likely to approve orphan-drug applications more quickly than nonorphan-drug applications, which sharply reduces costs for the orphan-drug manufacturer, increasing its economic returns, as Figure 3.10 shows.

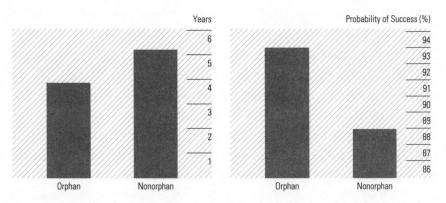

Figure 3.10   Speed of Regulatory Approval and Probability of Success for Orphan and Nonorphan Drugs
Note: Approval times are measured from launch of Phase II trials to commercial drug launch.
Source: Drug Discovery Today.

On the flip side, how can you tell if a moat based on efficient scale is eroding? Be on the lookout for markets that were once served efficiently by one company that can now be served efficiently by multiple companies. The telecom industry is a good example. Take Telecom Corporation of New Zealand. Like American telecom carriers up until the 1980s, New Zealand telecoms had local monopolies because regulators assumed that encouraging competition in the market meant stringing multiple sets of wires and telephone poles across the country, which would be wasteful and inefficient. In the early 2000s, the New Zealand government gradually deregulated the industry, believing that New Zealanders were paying too much for inadequate services versus other developed nations. The resulting influx of new competitors into the market such as TelstraClear (now part of Vodafone), Orcon, 2degrees, and ihug caused New Zealand Telecom's mobile market share to decline to 32% in mid-2012 from 68% in late 1999. We expect more competitors to continue to enter the market, putting pressure on market shares and overall economic returns. In short, when regulators decide that a market can be efficiently served by multiple competitors versus a single company, you likely have a negative moat trend.

Best Practices for Moat Trend Analysis

We've covered a lot of specific examples meant to help you see all that goes into evaluating moat trends. Here's a summary checklist to help you remember some of the key questions to consider for each moat source.

- Identify the moat source (or sources) for the firm.
    Ask the following questions and be able to explain why the changes are occurring.
- General and quantitative trend questions:
    - Is the company taking or losing market share within its industry?
    - Are midcycle operating margins higher or lower than today's levels?
    - Are incremental ROICs markedly higher or lower than current levels?
    - Is the sector growing or shrinking as a proportion of the overall industry's profit pool?
    - What do pricing trends look like?
    - What are the large opportunities and threats the firm is facing? Are there opportunities for the firm to extend its existing advantages into a

new product category or market? Conversely, are barriers to entry for the firm's existing markets declining, placing the firm at risk of being disrupted by new entrants?

- Qualitative trend questions by moat source.
  - Cost advantage:
    - Are suppliers increasing their bargaining power or not? Can the firm pass through supplier charges in a timely and efficient manner?
    - Why are the trends within a company's cost structure different than peers and the industry going forward? Is it a unique process?
    - Are there substitutes or complementary products that could change the cost/value equation?
  - Network effects:
    - What level of engagement does each user have with the network or marketplace? Is the engagement increasing or declining?
    - Can customers obtain similar benefits by being part of multiple networks, or is the market designed to support a single winner-take-all market? Are competitors starting up their own networks?
    - How is the company capturing the value of each incremental node added to its network? Can users duplicate the network by partnering with each other, cutting out the middleman?
  - Switching costs:
    - Are technological improvements disrupting the industry and lowering overall switching costs?
    - Are contract terms lengthening or shortening?
    - How customized is the company's product for a given application? Is the level of customization within the industry increasing or not?
  - Intangibles:
    - Are customers growing more or less willing to pay up for a firm's brand? If the brand is based on reputation, social cachet, or another type of emotional connection, are the factors that are affecting a brand's perception growing more or less important?
    - If the firm's intangible-based trend is built around patents, how easy is it to design around the patents? What are the trends in R&D productivity in terms of annual patent grants, customer licenses for the developed technology, or overall drug approval rates?

- Are there learning-curve benefits in the industry?
- Efficient scale:
  - How is the company's relationship with its regulators?
  - Are new technologies, markets, or other developments encouraging regulators to reconsider their original regulatory assumptions?
  - Looking at anticipated growth rates for the market, will it become easier or harder for new entrants to break into the larger market over time?

How Stewardship Affects Economic Moats

Contributed by Todd Wenning, who oversees Morningstar's equity stewardship methodology

Over time, the skill with which a company's managers allocate capital has an enormous impact on the enterprise's value.
—*Berkshire Hathaway, 1994 shareholder letter*

Prudent capital allocation is more important today than ever before. Even for successful firms that have made it to the corporate mountaintop, rapid technological advances, globalization, and the relentless pursuit of economic profits have dramatically shortened the length of time companies can expect to remain on top. According to consulting firm Innosight, the average lifespan for an S&P 500 component has shrunk from 61 years in 1958 to 25 years in 1980 to just 18 years in 2011. In this increasingly Darwinian corporate landscape, then, it's absolutely critical to understand how effectively a company's management team allocates shareholder capital toward moat-widening projects and investments while balancing returns of shareholder cash through buybacks and dividends.

Meet Our Stewardship Methodology

At Morningstar, analyzing how effectively a company's management team allocates its capital is at the heart of our stewardship methodology. We have long believed that effective management cannot constitute a moat in and of itself, because we're looking for structural attributes of the underlying business when assigning moat ratings, and by definition, a great management team could walk out the door, leaving the business without a sustainable competitive advantage. While strong management itself cannot be the source of an economic moat, we believe management's capital-allocation decisions can lead to the establishment, enhancement, or erosion of a moat. Put another way, we want to better understand the intersection of management and moat with each company we research.

While the purpose of our stewardship ratings has always been to indicate how well management teams are acting on shareholders' behalf, in mid-2011 we improved the methodology behind our ratings. Initially, we used a "check-the-box" grading system of corporate governance practices, but we found this was not a foolproof predictor of good capital-allocation decision-making and creation of shareholder value. Indeed, we found a number of companies with poor corporate governance practices that exhibited exceptionally strong capital allocation, and vice versa. Based on our previous methodology, for example, Ford carried a very low stewardship grade due primarily to some poor corporate governance practices such as having two share classes, but we believe CEO Alan Mulally has done a fine job allocating shareholder capital since taking the job in 2006. Further, we found that what's considered "good" corporate governance can vary quite a bit across global markets, which made it hard to compare the stewardship of two companies based in different parts of the world.

Our new and improved stewardship methodology focuses less on box-checking and more on management's track record on activities like investment strategy, investment timing and valuation, the use of financial leverage, dividend and share-buyback policies, execution, compensation, related-party transactions, and accounting practices. We find these factors not only to be more universally applicable for comparing stewardship across global markets, but also to better reveal how well management teams are allocating shareholder capital to build or enhance economic moats.

When evaluating management track records, we're always mindful that some results—particularly over the short term—have more to do with luck than skill. Just as an investor can take all of the right steps in evaluating a stock only to have the market nosedive or have another unforeseen event hamper performance, a management team can make great decisions and still experience bad near-term results. As Michael Mauboussin puts it in his book *The Success Equation: Untangling Skill and Luck in Business, Sports, and Investing*, "When a measure of luck is involved, a good process will have a good outcome but only *over time*." Realizing that luck will come and go, we want to hone in on the thoroughness of management's investment evaluation process and determine whether recent successes and failures have altered that process. This, we believe, tells us more about the quality of the firm's general capital-allocation decisions than whatever short-term results might suggest.

Our goal when evaluating stewardship is to understand how well a management team has played the hand it's been dealt. Rather than just using hindsight to determine how a particular decision panned out, we really try to put ourselves in management's shoes at the time a decision was made. In assessing the thought process behind management's decision to acquire another company, start a joint venture, invest in capital expenditures, or repurchase stock, we want to know:

- What other options did management have at the time?
- How did the timing of the decision fall in the industry's cycle?
- What were the prevailing industry valuations at the time an acquisition or divestment was announced?

After thoroughly reviewing a company's capital-allocation track record and process for evaluating new investments, we assign its managers one of three stewardship ratings: Exemplary, Standard, or Poor. In Table 4.1, you can see the current distribution of these ratings as well as brief explanations for each rating.

Drilling Down

Now that we've explored some of the broad stewardship themes, let's take a closer look at how we view some of the common capital-allocation factors.

Table 4.1   Stewardship Rating Distribution and Descriptions

Rating	% of Total Ratings	Description
Standard	84	Most of the companies in our coverage universe receive our default Standard stewardship rating due either to an absence of evidence that managers have made exceptionally strong or poor capital-allocation decisions, or because the net result of the decisions has been approximately neutral to shareholder value.
Exemplary	9	Exemplary stewards of shareholder capital tend to have a history of value-accretive acquisitions, optimal financial leverage, ideal dividend and share-buyback policies, and investments that enhance competitive advantages. Exemplary stewards are also more focused on creating long-term shareholder value even if it comes at the expense of short-term results. A good litmus test for an Exemplary rating is to ask, "Is this a candidate for CEO or CFO of the year?"
Poor	7	Poor stewards of shareholder capital are more likely to display highly inappropriate financial leverage from an equityholder's perspective, a track record of value-destructive investments (goodwill impairment is one piece of evidence), and frequent operational, strategic, and execution-related missteps.

SOURCE: Morningstar analysis.

Investment Strategy and Valuation

When you boil it down, companies have three basic options when they're deciding what to do with their capital: They can reinvest cash in the business, save it, or return it to claimholders.

Reinvesting in the business, through either expending capital or acquiring other companies, is the primary use of shareholder capital for most businesses. When thinking about reinvestment, bear in mind that expanding the size of the business is often in management's best interest because the bigger the company gets, the larger remuneration package management can command. We're certainly not against growth, but we want to make sure it's the right kind of growth that's occurring—that is, value-enhancing, moat-widening growth rather than growth that boosts short-term results to the detriment of long-term value.

A key question to ask when analyzing any company is, "Has the firm strayed from core competencies in its pursuit of growth?" All else equal, we prefer to see companies stick to what they know best. A firm with Exemplary stewardship will be one that has consistently made investments in projects that establish or enhance its core business and competitive advantages. Similarly, we look favorably on management teams with a track record of shedding noncore or underperforming assets at good-to-fair prices. For example, spirits company Brown-Forman has earned an Exemplary stewardship rating thanks in part to its decision to make key divestments of noncore business lines—consumer durables in 2007 and various wine brands in 2009 and 2011—which has helped the firm focus and consistently generate returns well above its cost of capital.

Firms that frequently engage in projects or deals outside of their core competencies sometimes justify the actions as a means to "diversify" operations or to reduce cyclicality in the business. But these deals can harm investors in two ways. First, you can typically diversify your portfolio much more cheaply on your own using other securities. Second, such deals increase the odds of unwelcome surprises, worse-than-expected synergies, and culture clashes between the merged companies. Companies may also pursue noncore acquisitions as a means to boost short-term growth with less regard for long-term value creation. An example of this was packaging company Sealed Air's $4.3 billion acquisition of cleaning products firm Diversey in 2011. The strategic rationale for the deal was tenuous at best, given the lack of overlap between packaging and cleaning services, and to make matters worse, Sealed Air diluted shareholders and dangerously leveraged its balance sheet to finance the deal. Almost immediately after the deal was announced, several executives—two from Diversey and one from Sealed Air—resigned and Sealed Air's largest shareholder sold off the vast majority of its once 30%-plus stake in the company. Just a year after the deal was consummated, Sealed Air took a $1.2 billion impairment charge on the Diversey acquisition and left Sealed Air's balance sheet highly leveraged.

Finally, even if a company has consistently invested in entities that make good strategic sense, it can still be a poor allocator of shareholder capital if it pays too much for the deals. As Warren Buffett and Charlie Munger put it in the 2011 Berkshire Hathaway shareholder letter, "The first law of capital allocation—whether the money is slated for acquisitions or share repurchases—is that what is smart at one price is dumb at another." No matter how good an investment or acquisition may seem, paying $1.20 for $1 worth of assets won't enhance shareholder value. Firms worthy of Exemplary stewardship ratings will avoid bidding wars that often result in a "winner's curse," make contrarian or countercyclical investments, and be willing to walk away from deals that don't make financial sense.

Execution

Our stewardship methodology doesn't punish companies for a string of bad luck alone. Instead, we're more interested in how management's actions may have played a role in value-destructive events. A classic recent example is oil giant BP, where a consistently poor safety record resulted in massive legal liabilities and cleanup costs that contributed to significant shareholder value destruction.

Some companies are also keen on setting out aggressive medium-term growth and profitability targets at analyst gatherings or well-attended conferences, which can boost investor sentiment in the short run. If management can execute on those targets, that's great, but firms that overpromise and underdeliver apparently don't understand their businesses well, can quickly lose credibility with investors and analysts, and won't be taken as seriously next time around.

Financial Leverage

Management's decisions regarding capital structure can have a profound impact on shareholder returns, uncertainty, and volatility. Be wary of firms with leverage ratios that are inappropriate for their lines of business. For example, firms that operate in highly cyclical, capital-intensive industries should avoid carrying a large debt load, as it can exaggerate the inherent volatility in the business and put shareholders' equity at risk. Similarly, firms that carry no debt, yet have few reinvestment needs and operate in stable and mature industries, may not be maximizing shareholder value, as issuing debt could lower the firm's cost of capital. Exemplary stewards of shareholder capital tend to consistently strike the right balance of debt and equity financing.

Dividend and Share-Buyback Policies

Ideally, firms will reinvest in their business up to the point where they are no longer generating economic profit and then return the remaining cash to shareholders via cash dividends and share repurchases. Exemplary stewards will have dividend and share-buyback policies that follow a "Goldilocks" principle of not too much, not too little, but just right. As much as we don't like to see companies borrow in an effort to sustain unsustainable dividend or buyback policies, we also don't want to see firms hoarding too much cash or engaging in "empire building" behavior.

The ideal dividend policy will vary by company, but the common traits should be consistency, affordability, and transparency.

- Consistency: A company's board may choose to employ target payout or coverage ratios, pay regular or special dividends, or aim to increase payouts in line with earnings, but you ultimately want a reliable policy that won't be frequently altered to match the prevailing business environment.
- Affordability: A dividend policy should leave enough cash for management to reinvest in value-enhancing projects and should bear some relationship to the company's performance over the longer term. Firms in cyclical industries should, all else equal, pay out a smaller percentage of their earnings than firms in defensive industries. In other words, as the predictability of annual profits decreases, a larger margin of safety should be built into the firm's desired payout ratio, and vice versa.
- Transparency: We think firms that are intent on distributing a significant amount of their annual earnings as dividends should have an established dividend policy that's outlined in the annual report.

Over the past 20 years, share repurchases have become an increasingly popular way for companies to return shareholder cash. Ideally, firms will repurchase stock only when the shares are trading at a discount to intrinsic value, but we've also found that some firms employ buybacks for less palatable reasons—for instance, to manage earnings per share or offset the dilutive effects of employee stock options with little regard for the price paid. A prime example of a buyback policy gone wrong was Hewlett-Packard, which spent about $10 billion a year on average on share repurchases between fiscal years 2006 and 2011 at prices that were, in hindsight, well above the company's intrinsic value. Compared with firms that focus on opportunistically buying back stock at a discount to fair value, we're less enthusiastic about firms that take a "dollar-cost averaging" approach to buybacks. These firms repurchase large amounts of stock each year hoping to return cash near fair value over time. Still, we recognize that repurchases near fair value can at times be a better use of capital than overpaying for an acquisition.

Despite the increasing use of buybacks as a means of returning shareholder cash, we find surprisingly few examples of firms with established buyback policies that are also clearly communicated to shareholders. Dividend policies and general mergers and acquisitions, or M&A, strategies, on the other hand, are far more frequently disseminated to shareholders. One notable exception is U.K.-based retailer Next, which spent two full pages of its 2012 annual report outlining its buyback philosophy. We wish more companies would follow Next's example and more thoroughly explain their buyback policies.

Compensation

Our stewardship methodology considers the relative size of a company's executive compensation package, but this factors into our rating only if we believe it will have a positive or negative effect on capital-allocation decisions. An excessive CEO pay package may be indicative of a situation in which one man or woman has too much control over internal decisions. As legendary investor Philip Fisher described it in his book *Common Stocks and Uncommon Profits*, "If the salary of the number-one man is very much larger than that of the next two or three, a warning flag is flying." For example, we look unfavorably on GAMCO Investors because of chairman, chief executive officer, portfolio manager, and chief investment officer Mario Gabelli's outsize pay package, which in 2012 amounted to $70.9 million or about 20% of the company's annual revenue.

Instead, we prefer to see executive cash compensation based on metrics that motivate the leadership team to invest in value-enhancing and moat-enhancing projects. It's also important that compensation schemes incorporate long-term performance. After all, many wise strategic investments require up to several years of capital expenditures, research and development, or R&D, investments, or marketing costs before payoff. If managers are motivated to boost only short-term earnings and cash flows, they might actually forgo value-creating projects because doing so would avoid near-term expenses.

Ball Corporation's annual cash bonuses, for example, are based on year-over-year growth in economic value added, or EVA—a metric calculated by taking net operating profit after tax and subtracting a cost of capital charge. Ball's longer-term cash incentives are primarily based on returns on invested capital relative to the board's target "hurdle rate." In other words, Ball management isn't rewarded for simply increasing the size of the business; it earns a bonus only if the company is generating economic profits. We believe metrics such as EVA and returns on invested capital are particularly attractive as they are closely related to the state of the company's competitive advantages and better align management's economic interests with those of long-term shareholders.

Related-Party Transactions

Related-party transactions, in which a company's business deals occur with parties that have outside relationships with company managers or owners, generally do not play a large factor in determining our stewardship ratings. We would be inclined, however, to place a Poor stewardship rating on companies that frequently redirect value to friends and family at the expense of shareholders.

Accounting Practices

A history of deceitful accounting practices is most certainly grounds for a Poor stewardship rating. Famous accounting scandals such as Enron, WorldCom, and Tyco, however, stand out precisely because such massive fraud is relatively rare among large publicly traded companies. Far more common are aggressive accounting practices that can place poor capital-allocation decisions in a better light. Exemplary stewards of shareholder capital will usually have a track record of transparency and consistency when it comes to accounting practices. We also prefer to see firms use reasonable estimates for important accounting assumptions related to items like pensions, depreciation, and revenue recognition.

Management Backgrounds

We assess the backgrounds of a company's managers and consider whether they're a good fit for their positions. Factors such as relevant and sufficient experience influence our consideration here, as well as a manager's track record in previous jobs and any external factors that may have played a role in that leader's previous successes or failures.

Health, Safety, and Environment

As fellow citizens of the planet, we care about how corporations treat their employees, their communities, and the environment. But once we put on our equity analyst hats and turn to stewardship ratings, we are forced to be more clinical. Our stewardship ratings are meant to measure one thing and one thing only: how a company's managers behave on behalf of shareholders. And because we assess stewardship from a shareholder—not a stakeholder—perspective, our default stance on a company's health, safety, and environment, or HSE, practices is agnostic. As citizens of the planet, the fact that our stewardship ratings may turn a blind eye to nefarious HSE practices may make us queasy. But to be true to the purpose of the rating, we must restrict our consideration to a shareholder-value perspective. That said, if a company's HSE record has had a demonstrated impact on operational performance or shareholder value, then we take that into consideration in our assessment of stewardship of shareholder capital.

Ownership Structure

Who owns the company? It's a simple question, but it can reveal a lot about why management and the board are making certain decisions. When analyzing a company's ownership structure, we consider the extent (if any) of family or insider ownership, government ownership, and significant stakes owned by other companies. We also look for different share classes with unequal voting classes. Certain structures can reduce the power of minority shareholders, but we don't consider them cause for concern by themselves. Indeed, the controlling shareholders' economic interests might be significantly aligned with those of minority shareholders. Conversely, we consider it a sign of poor stewardship when ownership structures lead to or influence value-destructive decisions at the expense of minority shareholders.

Stakeholder Focus

Though Morningstar's stewardship methodology is firmly focused on shareholders, some jurisdictions require corporations to act in the interests of all stakeholders, not just shareholders. Germany, for example, requires employee representation on many corporate boards. Many Japanese companies maintain ownership positions in their suppliers and customers, which could be perceived as generating conflicts of interest. Having a stakeholder focus written into the articles of incorporation, or counting suppliers and customers among the shareholders, isn't necessarily bad news for shareholders, though. In some cases, employee representation on the board may lead to better coordination for companies with complex processes, so the German model may give some companies an advantage. And crossholdings with customers and suppliers may have the effect of reducing transaction costs by creating virtual integration along the value chain, so perhaps the Japanese model makes sense in some cases. So, our process is to take note when a company has a stakeholder focus and when that focus has led to actions for or against the interest of shareholders.

Communication With Shareholders

Executives who have made it to the top of the corporate ladder are usually highly skilled communicators who have a vested interest in painting their results in a positive light. As such, investors are often left to read between the lines of veiled management communications—particularly when the business falls on hard times. We appreciate when executives own up to strategic missteps and are forthcoming about challenges the company faces. Being communicative with shareholders when times are bad can also make management's words more believable when times are good. Conversely, we don't like to see companies with a record of realigning reporting segments every few years, as this can serve to sweep poorly performing businesses under the rug and make it difficult for investors to assess capital-allocation decisions.

Stewardship Ratings by Moat and Sector

Morningstar analysts have assigned stewardship ratings to more than 1,100 companies across the global markets. Through this collective effort, we've gained some valuable insights into how stewardship relates to economic moats and sectors.

For starters, let's take a look at Figure 4.1, which illustrates the stewardship rating distribution by economic moat rating.

As you can see, Morningstar analysts have awarded Exemplary stewardship ratings to a greater percentage of wide-moat companies than to narrow-moat companies and to more narrow-moat companies than no-moat companies.

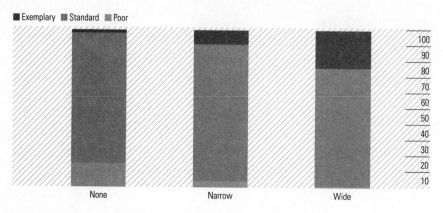

Figure 4.1   Stewardship Ratings by Economic Moat Rating (%)
SOURCE: Morningstar analysis.

The opposite is true for Poor stewardship ratings. Though there's potentially a "halo effect" at work here whereby our analysts' favorable view of a company's competitive advantages biases our view of management's skill, and vice versa, we believe there are at least three explanations for this positive correlation between moat and stewardship ratings.

1. Management skill: Management itself can't make a moat, but a company can enhance or establish a moat resulting from its management's skillful efforts to allocate capital toward moat-widening projects. On the other hand, poor stewards of shareholder capital that consistently invest in competitively disadvantaged projects for the sake of short-term growth and destroy long-term shareholder value in the process would likely see moats erode over time.

2. Magnet effect: Companies with sustainable competitive advantages are often able to better attract or retain outstanding managers and managers-to-be than firms without economic moats.

3. Chasing their tails: Try as they might, managers of no-moat firms may simply lack moat-widening investment opportunities because of industry realities (think of buggy whip manufacturers heavily investing in new capacity after the automobile was commercialized). They may nevertheless feel the need to do something—anything—to keep the company growing even if it doesn't make economic sense to do so. This can lead management to embark on large acquisitions of unrelated companies, pursue far-out growth

initiatives, or sell off still-valuable assets on the cheap. This phenomenon might explain the higher percentage of Poor stewardship ratings for no-moat companies versus those for wide- or narrow-moat companies.

We also gain some insights by breaking out stewardship ratings by sector, as in Figure 4.2.

By viewing stewardship ratings this way, we can better understand that the importance of capital-allocation decisions varies by sector. For example, the highest percentage of nonstandard stewardship ratings lies in the energy and financial services sectors. Intuitively, this makes sense, as energy and financial companies' managers make frequent and meaningful capital-allocation and strategic decisions. At energy companies, managers must decide where to invest cash flows from producing wells, and portfolio shifts can have a meaningful impact on the overall competitive position of the firm. For example, companies like ExxonMobil and Chevron have assembled portfolios of high-quality energy assets by maintaining a strategy of pursuing high-return opportunities. For financial firms, balance-sheet strategy and loan underwriting standards have a material effect on growth, risk, and profitability. For example, U.S. Bancorp could have pursued aggressive growth by loosening its loan underwriting standards, but its culture includes sound underwriting practices, and as a result the bank never incurred a loss even at the height of the financial crisis. Both of these sectors also face frequent capital needs, where the skill (or lack thereof) of management can have a meaningful impact.

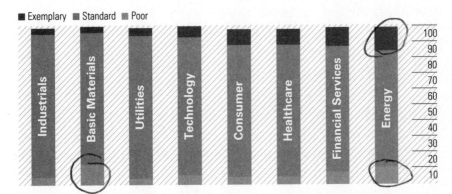

Figure 4.2 Stewardship Ratings by Sector (%)
SOURCE: Morningstar analysis.

The primary factors separating extraordinarily good and bad stewards of shareholder capital also differ by sector. In the utilities sector, for example, successful navigation of the regulatory landscape is the primary differentiator, while in the consumer sector, brand investments and execution are the main considerations separating successful management teams from those who lead their companies astray.

To further illustrate, let's take a closer look at some examples of exemplary and poor stewardship in each sector.

Basic Materials

Common themes are investment strategy and valuation, and financial leverage.

Exemplary Standout: Eldorado Gold Eldorado is the only company in our gold mining coverage universe that has earned an economic moat, which is largely attributable to CEO Paul Wright and his management team amassing a portfolio of low-cost, long-life mining assets without paying dearly for them. Wright has accomplished this by focusing on under-the-radar mining jurisdictions such as China, Turkey, and Greece (where the competition for quality mining assets is less intense), as well as through prudent capital allocation. Indeed, Eldorado has largely avoided large, dilutive acquisitions—a common destroyer of returns in the gold mining industry—and instead has focused on using its geological expertise to internally explore and develop gold mining assets. The company is also committed to rewarding shareholders and in October 2011 initiated a gold-price-linked dividend scheme that will increase its dividend when gold prices rise. The move makes Eldorado one of only two gold miners to link its dividend to gold prices, and we think the scheme benefits shareholders by limiting capital available for reinvestment when gold prices are peaking and by granting equity investors greater leverage to gold prices.

Poor Standout: Stora Enso Finnish pulp and paper company Stora Enso switched reporting segments twice in less than two years, which we find worrisome. In April 2013, Stora Enso announced that it would consolidate its existing four reporting segments into three by combining its building and living segment with its printing and reading segment—two businesses with very little in common. Just 15 months earlier, Stora Enso had completely reworked its reporting structure and combined three separate paper reporting segments to create that printing and reading segment. Reducing the transparency of such an important line of business as paper and reading (40% of 2012 sales) is not a shareholder-friendly move, in our opinion. Stora also has two share classes—A and R—that carry the same dividend but different voting rights. Each A share equals one vote at shareholder meetings while each R share equals a one-tenth vote. The top four shareholders control nearly 70% of the voting power. We don't consider Stora's dual share-class structure very shareholder-friendly, as R-share owners have less say on matters of corporate policy.

Consumer

Common themes are strategy execution, brand investments, and balanced growth strategies.

Exemplary Standout: Coca-Cola Coca-Cola is led by exemplary stewards. We attribute the firm's consistent execution in the difficult operating environment of the past several years to strong leadership and a very deep bench of executive talent. We are also impressed by management's focus on the company's "2020 Vision" initiative, which emphasizes making the best decisions to expand the business over the long term, not just the next quarter. Coca-Cola and its bottling partners are consistently investing behind their brands to maintain their premium positioning, as well as steadily building out their manufacturing and distribution capabilities to maintain Coca-Cola's global leadership position in the nonalcoholic ready-to-drink category.

Poor Standout: Dean Foods We think Dean Foods' stewardship of shareholder capital is Poor. Management's ill-timed decision to saddle the firm with debt in order to pay a special dividend to shareholders in 2007 only increased the volatility inherent in Dean's results during the past several years. Debt paydown and cost improvement have been a top focus for the dairy processor of late; however, we aren't convinced that management has learned its lesson. Dean recently completed the spin-off of its high-growth, high-margin WhiteWave-Alpro business and sold its Morningstar (no relation) food business, utilizing the proceeds to reduce leverage further. Although this is a positive given that leverage should decline, Dean's debt could still be difficult to service without the more stable and higher-profit levels that the WhiteWave-Alpro segment generates (as compared with Dean's legacy business).

Energy

Common themes are portfolio construction decisions and execution.

Exemplary Standout: National Oilwell Varco CEO Merrill (Pete) Miller Jr. has led National Oilwell Varco since 2001 and was Morningstar's 2012 CEO of the Year. In late 2012, Miller stepped back from the day-to-day operations of NOV in preparation for his eventual retirement. After orchestrating numerous acquisitions that have largely consolidated the equipment market to the firm's benefit, Miller has earned his paycheck, in our opinion. The company also consistently offers some of the best industry commentary on its quarterly calls. We believe Miller and recently elevated COO Clay Williams, who now manages more of the day-to-day operations, are shrewd judges of value and very good capital allocators. We think the acquisitions of several firms in recent years will expand National Oilwell Varco's footprint in key growth areas and will create shareholder value over the long run. Overall, we view National Oilwell Varco as a very well-run company with a thoughtful management team that is focused on creating shareholder value.

Poor Standout: Weatherford International Despite a wealth of opportunity for oil-services firms like Weatherford International, the company has struggled operationally over the past few years and lost ground to peers. For example, the firm has restated its financials three times in recent years because of tax issues, which ultimately led to the resignation of its CFO; it overinvested in its international infrastructure from 2007 to 2008, which led to numerous write-offs in 2010 and 2011; and it has struggled with major projects in Mexico, the Middle East, and North Africa. Unlike Halliburton and Schlumberger, Weatherford has been unable to achieve a high level of consistent service quality or to offer a robust enough product portfolio to make it a preferred services vendor. As a result, we believe Weatherford has to consistently price its services at a discount to the industry leaders. By most shareholder metrics, Weatherford has failed to deliver value to shareholders over the past few years, and the management team struggles with effective capital allocation.

Financial Services

Common themes are balance sheet decisions, underwriting standards, and growth strategies.

Exemplary Standout: T. Rowe Price This investment firm's management committee, which is responsible for guiding, implementing, and reviewing major policy and operating initiatives, has done an exemplary job over the years. Capital allocation has been prudent, with the company carrying little to no debt on its books, engaging in very little acquisition activity, and tending to return cash to shareholders in the form of dividends and share repurchases. In the asset-management industry, debt can be a net negative. We saw this during the financial crisis when several firms that were carrying larger levels of debt had to scramble to raise capital (including issuing additional equity) after revenue and profitability dropped dramatically in response to the market decline.

Poor Standout: Nomura Holdings We think investment bank Nomura has exhibited Poor stewardship of shareholder capital. The company has cycled through several CEOs in the past two decades. Koji Nagai is the most recent to head the company, replacing Kenichi Watanabe following an insider trading scandal. In the past, management's capital allocation left much to be desired. Returns on equity seldom exceeded 10% over the past decade, and a massive fiscal 2009 loss and subsequent capital raise resulted in significant shareholder dilution.

Healthcare

Common themes are execution and M&A discipline.

Exemplary Standout: Sanofi Sanofi's increasingly wise deployment of capital has led us to boost the company's stewardship rating to Exemplary. Since Chris Viehbacher took over as CEO in late 2008, the company's major acquisitions and use of capital have generated strong returns and increased its competitive position. From an acquisition standpoint, the Medley, Chattem, Merial, and Genzyme acquisitions all have generated returns on capital employed above the weighted average cost of capital within fewer than four years. Additionally, the Genzyme acquisition shows how Sanofi avoided overpaying for the company (a typical big-pharma error) by using contingent value rights, or CVR, to appease Genzyme. Further, Viehbacher's decision to significantly cut underperforming pipeline drugs early in his tenure has led to a much stronger pipeline and less wasted capital along the way.

Poor Standout: PerkinElmer We assign PerkinElmer a Poor stewardship grade, as the executive team so far has a very pedestrian record when it comes to value creation and shareholder returns. The company has deployed all of its free cash from operations (and had to increase its debt level) into acquisitions, which have yet to produce a meaningful contribution to returns. Although we favor the strategic shift away from cyclical product lines, results have nonetheless been subpar, particularly when compared with many peers in analytical instrumentation. Admittedly, the last recession cycle disrupted PerkinElmer's strategy, but the company now has had a decade of stagnant operating margins and only in half of those years has it managed to (barely) exceed its cost of capital, including goodwill. Meanwhile, the dividend has stayed unchanged, and we believe the company could have done a better job buying back its shares when we considered them undervalued.

Industrials

Common themes are execution, employee relationships, and investment strategy and valuation.

Exemplary Standout: Rockwell Automation Under the current management team's guidance, Rockwell has moved away from purely being a discrete controls component business to become a respectable competitor in multidisciplinary controls, lifting shareholder returns in the process. In the first few years of the 21st century, Rockwell made the strategic decision to invest in technology that would allow it not only to provide more value to existing customers, but also to extend the company's reach into new markets. Shareholders own a more competitively advantaged company today than they did 10 years ago. In our opinion, this is largely due to the decision making of the leadership team, leading to our exemplary Stewardship rating.

Poor Standout: Siemens Considering Siemens' strong portfolio and decent competitive positioning, we have been somewhat discouraged by the electronics and engineering firm's inability to drive strong profitability and, subsequently, returns on invested capital. A history of impairments and poor operational execution cloud our opinion of the firm and detract from the ultimate valuation. While these factors are reparable, our Poor stewardship rating reflects a company whose management team has not done enough to create long-term shareholder value. In spite of a change at the helm, we continue to view Siemens' stewardship as Poor, though successful execution and operating improvement may adjust our thinking.

Technology

Common themes are innovation success/failure, execution, and investment strategy and valuation.

Exemplary Standout: IBM IBM's management team has adroitly navigated the secular trend toward distributed open-standards computing by diversifying its hardware platforms, broadening its software portfolio, and building a formidable services organization. The result has been solid long-term financial performance. Since 2002, IBM's revenue, gross profit, and operating profit have compounded at annual rates of 3%, 6%, and 12%, respectively, while returns on invested capital have remained firmly above the company's cost of capital. Other technology firms have grown faster over the past decade, but few can point to a track record that is as consistent or shareholder friendly as IBM's.

Poor Standout: BlackBerry At the time of this writing, BlackBerry was a company on life support, unlikely to ever be a profitable stand-alone smartphone marker and instead searching for any way to reduce its cash burn, monetize its variety of assets, or outright sell part or all of the company. BlackBerry's missteps came years ago, when the firm failed to identify and properly respond to the threat of web-enabled smartphones that offered robust app stores and developer support, such as Apple's iOS and Google's Android platform. BlackBerry's first full-touchscreen device, the BlackBerry Storm, was a flop, and the firm was unable to develop a compelling alternative to these devices thereafter. BlackBerry 10 encountered several delays and was launched after the holiday season in 2013, allowing more potential customers to gravitate to other devices. Although BB10 devices have some interesting features and gestures, and we view the operating system as solid, the firm's efforts appear to be too little, too late. Under new CEO John Chen, BlackBerry's best chance for survival may come as a software or services company, but we don't see the firm ever regaining its former glory in the smartphone space.

Utilities

Common themes are relationships with regulators, shareholder return policies.

Exemplary Standout: Southern Management has fostered excellent regulatory relations in this utility's service territory—a fundamental driver of a regulated utility's moat—earning premium returns on equity and higher ROICs than most regulated peers. Further, management has operated Southern's nonregulated business very conservatively, consistently earning returns on capital in line with its regulatory allowed returns. Southern doesn't appear to engage in aggressive accounting, and executive compensation is roughly in line with that of its peer group. We think the fact that many high-level executives running other utilities trace their roots to Southern is testament to the firm's positive corporate culture.

Poor Standout: Enersis This Latin American utility's ownership structure is complex. Enel, the Italian integrated energy company, owns 92.1% of Endesa Spain, which owns 60.6% of Enersis. Formerly Italy's state-owned monopoly electric utility, Enel was partially privatized, and the Italian state retains a 31.2% stake in Enel. Minority shareholders of Enersis have suffered from the natural conflicts of interest created by this structure. A $6 billion capital increase completed in 2013 diluted shareholders. Further, Enersis' management and board had supported an inflated valuation for the assets that Endesa contributed to the capital raise until Chilean regulators forced Enersis to obtain independent valuations.

5

Applying Moats to Dividend Investing

Contributed by Josh Peters, director of equity-income strategy for Morningstar and editor of the Morningstar® DividendInvestor SM newsletter

Our focus on economic moats and valuation doesn't directly address how companies deliver their total returns to shareholders—that is, we don't give extra credit for capital gains at the expense of dividends or vice versa. Because total return is the bottom line for all investors regardless of their strategic objectives or return preferences, it helps to stay agnostic on the question of income versus appreciation. This way, we can objectively evaluate any kind of situation set before us.

But even when we're talking in terms of total return, the question of "How?" is just as important for many investors as "How much?"

It might go without saying that some investors don't care for dividends. Perhaps it's a matter of taxes, which can be deferred on capital gains as long as the shareholder doesn't sell, while dividends (if not received in tax-deferred accounts like IRAs) trigger a tax liability with each payment. Some investors simply prefer growth for its own sake; with investing as with food, there's no reliable way to account for personal taste. A few market participants remain openly hostile to dividends; no one articulates this view more colorfully than venture capitalist and market commentator Andy Kessler:

> Dividends are just a bribe to get you interested in slow growing companies who can't be bothered to reinvest their earnings in something useful.
>
> —*Wall Street Journal*, "I Still Hate Dividends,
> Professor Siegel," Jan. 7, 2008

We must say we disagree with Mr. Kessler's view, as do a large and growing number of investors who have come to prioritize income over capital gains. For someone who is retired, or is soon to be, dividends offer a source of return that is always and only positive, paid out of companies that are generally (but not always) well established, financially stable, and less vulnerable to adverse economic and financial market conditions. Dividends are rarely the "bribe" that Kessler suggests; instead, we find that in most cases, they impose much-needed discipline on corporate officers and directors. Throw in the fact that dividend-paying stocks have a history of outperforming nonpayers, and that high-yielding stocks usually outperform low-yielding ones, and it becomes clear that dividends aren't just for over-the-hill companies or investors—dividends are for anyone interested in total return.

Yet Kessler's points, like the proverbial broken clock, are occasionally correct in specific circumstances. There's nothing inherently bad about a slow-growing company, as long as a big dividend rounds out a decent total return, but a complete absence of growth may well be a problem. We also frown on dividends that are so large that they starve a business of capital for expansion, but this more likely represents a capital-allocation or stewardship problem that goes beyond the dividend itself. And there are indeed a few dividends out there that we agree could be characterized fairly as bribes: those paid by mortgage REITs, business development companies, energy production partnerships, and the like. By paying large cash distributions, firms like these can lure unsuspecting investors into believing these speculative businesses are actually safe and steady income providers.

Our approach to dividend investing seeks to avoid these kinds of situations. Through Morningstar's *DividendInvestor* newsletter and its model portfolios, launched in January 2005, we've sought to deliver large, consistent, and growing streams of income as well as attractive long-term total returns. So far, our best tool for pursuing these objectives has been focusing on the concept of economic moats, which both protect the investor's dividend income and encourage that income to grow over time.

Why Dividends Matter

As we mentioned earlier, Morningstar's approach to investing does not explicitly consider the role of dividends relative to capital gains. Rather, using the insights gained about a particular business and its industry through the lens of long-term competitive positioning (aka moat building), we forecast future free cash flows and discount them back to the present-day dollars to arrive at a value for the shares. As that future unfolds, though, it's rare—and generally undesirable—for those future free cash flows to simply pile up on the company's balance sheet.

That practice, which we might call hoarding, is one of five basic avenues by which a company can handle its free cash flow. The others are: pay down debt or other obligations, acquire other businesses or assets, repurchase shares, and pay dividends. The question then becomes centered on which of these actions create or transmit value to shareholders in the most efficient manner.

Hoarding of cash has become commonplace since the financial crisis of 2008–09. While a hefty cash balance may be interpreted as a sign of financial health, it can also raise important questions about capital allocation. Many companies require at least some sizable amount of cash to deal with working-capital fluctuations; deeply cyclical businesses such as Ford and General Motors may also want to run up their cash balances during booms to reduce the probability of financial stress in the next downturn. However, to the extent that a swelling cash balance can be traced to these factors, it may not be fair to call this cash flow "free" if it isn't available to fund more direct returns to shareholders. In other cases, particularly among large multinational firms (Apple being the ultimate example), cash may be hoarded abroad to avoid paying higher U.S. income tax rates on foreign-sourced income. Setting aside the debate regarding corporate tax reform, investors should question the value of offshore cash balances and/or the quality of reported after-tax earnings if cash is not being repatriated in a way that benefits shareholders.

In several cases we've seen companies borrow in the domestic bond market to fund share repurchases or dividends rather than repatriate cash from abroad.

Debt reduction can be a good use of free cash flow if a company finds its balance sheet somewhat overextended—for example, after a large debt-financed acquisition. But if adverse circumstances (such as a secular decline in cash flow) lead to an excess of leverage, free cash flows that are devoted to reducing debt may have relatively little value for shareholders. The protracted decline of traditional telephone services, for example, has increased the effective leverage of landline-focused telecom firms like Frontier Communications. Using free cash flow to reduce debt is necessary for the long-run stability of the firm, but this benefits shareholders only in the sense that increased financial stress would be an even worse outcome.

Acquisitions can create value for shareholders, but eventual outcomes depend heavily on the capability of management to select, integrate, and manage acquired businesses effectively, as well as the price paid and the financing choices made. Many acquisitions fall into the category of "empire building," in which the benefits accrue to senior managers (who get paid more to run a larger enterprise) as well as the various bankers, lawyers, and consultants involved. Meanwhile, shareholders bear the risk. Then again, other firms have established good reputations as serial acquirers, ranging from industrial conglomerate Danaher to Warren Buffett's Berkshire Hathaway. We can't say that acquisitions are a good use of free cash flow across the board, nor a bad use, but they should be analyzed with considerable care.

Share repurchases have become an increasingly common mechanism by which free cash flows are remitted to a company's shareholders. In fact, in recent years, the dollar volume of share repurchases by members of the S&P 500 Index has exceeded the total outlay for dividends. By reducing the number of shares outstanding, each remaining share represents a larger percentage claim on the value of the business. However, this does not mean that each remaining share becomes more valuable: that depends on the price being paid. (Just ask the shareholders of serial repurchasers such as Dell and Hewlett-Packard.) Remember that cash—and therefore value—passes out of the company when shares are repurchased. Only if the price paid for the repurchased shares is less than the per-share value of the business has the repurchase increased the value of the remaining shares. Yet in practice, value is in the eye of the beholder, and it's not hard to imagine CEOs and CFOs overestimating what their company's shares are worth. Instead, repurchases are usually made when a company has excess cash flow—a condition usually correlating with above-average profits and share prices—rather than when its shares are cheap.

Paying dividends is the only cash flow redeployment option that provides direct and tangible returns to shareholders. Even when a company repurchases shares and touts that it's "returning cash to shareholders," it makes sense to ask, "Which shareholders?" Unlike the other four choices discussed earlier, where the impacts on shareholder value are circumstantial, a dividend cannot destroy value (unless the payment is so large that it could result in future financial distress, as in the case of a large special dividend funded by borrowing).

One may argue that a dividend cannot create value directly either, as it functions primarily as a vehicle for value that has already been created within the enterprise. Yet dividends have several positive consequences, including:

- Dividend payments provide investors with valuable signals regarding management's willingness to reward shareholders rather than just themselves. In a very real sense, dividends are a mark of corporate maturity, expressing through a check in the mail that the company's earning power is durable and its financial condition is strong.
- Dividends impose discipline on corporate managers. Once a regular dividend is established, the market expects that dividend to remain steady or increase over time. It isn't easy for a CEO to simply cancel the dividend because he or she has suddenly discovered a better use for the cash. By paying dividends rather than retaining 100% of earnings, officers and directors must (1) ration the remaining resources available for expansion with more care, which should focus capital outlays on higher-return uses, and (2) closely consider not just next quarter's profits, but the ability to meet the market's expectations for dividends far into the future—years, if not decades.
- An attractive and sustainable dividend policy can create a "clientele effect" in which shareholders, amply rewarded through dividends, are less likely to dump their shares and hurt the stock price on the basis of short-run fluctuations in profits. This in turn may give management a freer hand to concentrate on long-term initiatives, even at the expense of near-term profits or cash flow.

- Stocks that consistently offer high dividend yields—as long as those dividends are perceived to be sustainable—tend to fluctuate less than the overall market, leading to superior risk-adjusted returns.

This last point has been illustrated in numerous academic studies; one of our favorites is the data that Wharton professor Jeremy J. Siegel produced for his 2005 book, *The Future for Investors: Why the Tried and the True Triumph Over the Bold and the New.* We can also see this phenomenon in the long-term performance of several equity market indexes that focus on high-yielding stocks. In Figure 5.1 we see that one of the oldest, the Dow Jones U.S. Select Dividend Index, outperformed the S&P 500 Index by 3.2% annually between 1991 and 2012 with a monthly beta of 0.78. At first glance, you might attribute this performance to the decline of interest rates through this period. If this were the case, however, we should see rising valuations for the index expressed through falling dividend yields. That the trailing 12-month dividend yield on the index was very nearly the same in December 2012 as it was in December 1991 suggests that falling interest rates were not the cause of the outperformance.

If an otherwise attractive business does not pay a dividend, it's worth asking how its value is recognized by the market. As an investor's time horizon lengthens, the impact of dividends becomes more and more important—the combination of dividend yield and dividend growth explains 49% of the compound total return of the S&P 500 Index over the past 10 years, 83% over the

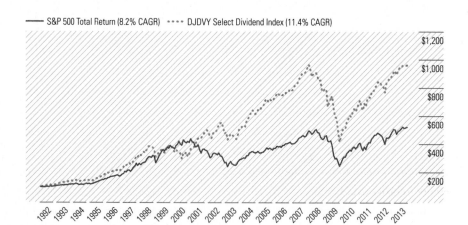

—— S&P 500 Total Return (8.2% CAGR)   ···· DJDVY Select Dividend Index (11.4% CAGR)

Figure 5.1 High-Yielding Stocks Outperform
NOTE: Compound value of $100 invested on Dec. 31, 1991.
SOURCE: Morningstar Direct℠.

past 20 years, and 91% over the past 100 years. But even for someone who isn't investing with the next century in mind, consider this. You have to lay out cash in order to purchase a share of stock. How does that share convert itself back into cash? The market provides a place to sell, but that cash isn't coming directly from the security itself. Stocks don't "mature" with a guaranteed return of principal the way bonds do, so the only underlying sources of cash are (1) cash tender offers or liquidations, akin to maturity events, and (2) cash dividends. Arbitrage between public markets and active private/strategic markets for business assets helps establish value for many businesses, but what about when a company is too big to be taken over—say, Google? If Google never pays a dividend and remains too big to be acquired, the only way an investor can realize cash from a position in Google is by selling shares on the open market. Ample dividends, by providing a tangible return independent of stock prices or transactions, allow shareholders to rely less on the stock market's daily popularity contest.

Which Dividends?

Earning good returns through dividends is a relatively straightforward exercise in leveraging the strengths of dividends themselves. Simply avoid dividends that are vulnerable to being cut (at any point in the foreseeable future), seek dividends that will grow, and pay reasonable or attractive prices when buying. This approach doesn't apply well to companies that don't pay significant or consistent dividends, but for those that do, you can organize your analysis of a company and its stock from the viewpoint of its dividend.

When considering a particular dividend-paying stock, ask three questions: Is the dividend safe? Will the dividend grow? What level of total return do future dividend prospects suggest? Although these three questions don't specifically deal with a company's economic moat or lack thereof, the moat is the essential context when evaluating the safety of a company's dividend and its ability to grow over time.

Consider the case of Clorox, a long-standing holding in one of *DividendInvestor*'s two model portfolios. If Clorox didn't have an economic moat, its dividend could hardly be considered sustainable, much less likely to grow over time.

In its 2013 fiscal year, which ended in June 2013, Clorox posted net income of $572 million, of which $337 million (59%) was paid out to shareholders through regular cash dividends, as shown in Table 5.1. Based on our calculations, the company earned a 25% return on invested capital for the year.

If Clorox had no economic moat—and therefore no ability to sustain profit margins at current levels in the face of future competition—we would expect the firm's long-run earning power to match its cost of capital, and probably sooner rather than later. Using an 8.0% cost of equity and 4.6% long-term cost of debt, we estimate Clorox's weighted average cost of capital at 7.7%. Assuming Clorox earned only that 7.7% weighted average cost of capital, its net income would have been only $117 million, 80% less than what the company actually earned, and 65% less than the sum of the dividends paid during the year.

Fortunately, Clorox does have strong evidence of an economic moat, which we trace to the firm's intangible assets—well-established brands like Hidden Valley (salad dressing), KC Masterpiece (barbeque sauce), Glad (trash bags), Kingsford (charcoal), Brita (water filters), and its namesake bleach and cleaning products. These brands enable Clorox to charge premium prices for its products, which, when combined with the firm's highly efficient manufacturing facilities, generate profit margins that rival competitors with substantially larger product portfolios. Yet Clorox rarely goes head-to-head with these giants; instead, it dominates relatively small niches.

Clorox's economic moat also plays a critical role in future dividend growth. The company routinely invests 2% of annual revenue in research and development and 4% of revenue in capital expenditures. If Clorox were investing in

Table 5.1 Clorox: Economic Moat Pays Dividends ($ Millions)

	2013 Actual	At WACC
Net Income	572	117
NOPAT	644	195
Average Invested Capital	2,569	2,569
Return on Invested Capital (%)	25.0	7.6
Dividends Paid	337	337
Dividends/Net Income (%)	59	288

NOTE: Net operating profit after tax (NOPAT) uses 34% tax rate.
SOURCE: Company filings, Morningstar.

areas where it didn't have competitive advantages—perhaps trying to develop, like Google, its own version of a self-driving car—we'd have little reason to expect these expenditures to earn adequate returns on capital or drive future increases in earnings per share or dividends. Instead, Clorox devotes its investment spending to developing new products and improving manufacturing efficiency within its moat-protected sandbox.

It would be fair to say that Clorox's opportunities for future growth are modest. Annual revenues, including the impact of several acquisitions and divestitures, rose only 3% a year on average between 2003 and 2013. There's little reason to think consumers will double their use of bleach overnight. But by concentrating its resources in moat-protected projects that have a high probability of generating attractive returns on capital, Clorox maximizes the value of its existing business and returns the bulk of remaining cash flows to shareholders, primarily through dividends. Thanks to earnings growth as well as an increasing payout ratio—which reflects not financial stresses but rather the company's ample ability and willingness to pay—Clorox raised its dividend an average of 11.4% annually between 2003 and 2013.

Pitney Bowes provides an excellent example of the same phenomenon at work in reverse. Anyone who has ever worked in a mailroom will recognize the name. Pitney has long had a near-monopoly on the U.S. postage meter market—a monopoly secured in large part by the fact that the U.S. Postal Service doesn't let just anyone print postage, as doing so is akin to printing money. However, what was once a wide economic moat began shrinking as postal volumes declined. Management compounded the problem by spending billions of dollars on acquisitions in adjacent but hardly moat-protected businesses, piling up a fair bit of debt along the way that only exacerbated the burden of a declining core business.

Until 2012, Pitney had a 30-year record of consecutive annual dividend hikes. However, as profits sagged, the dividend increases got smaller and smaller—strong evidence of a rapidly eroding moat. In early 2012, Pitney held its dividend flat. In early 2013, the dividend was chopped in half. But long before the dividend was actually reduced, the stock price had fallen sharply. The dividend was something of the bribe alluded to earlier, and even the bribe did not pay off.

It's hard to overstate the importance of avoiding dividend cuts. In the experience of *DividendInvestor*'s model portfolios through mid-2013, we've suffered

Table 5.2 Frequency and Magnitude of Dividend Cuts by Moat Rating

Moat Rating	Frequency of Cuts (%)	Average Cut Size (%)
No moat	7.4	69.8
Narrow moat	5.3	66.8
Wide moat	3.0	66.0

Source: Morningstar® Indexes.

negative total returns from 81% of the portfolio positions that reduced their dividends while we owned them (or shortly after a sale, by which time a dividend cut was reflected in the price). The only reason this metric isn't 100% is because three of the 16 stocks that handed us with dividend cuts were held until their dividend payments had recovered sharply. On the other hand, we've earned positive total returns 67% of the time from stocks that have had flat dividend rates while we've owned them (including several new positions as of this writing that haven't yet had time to raise their dividends) and an 89% win rate from stocks that have raised their dividends.

And how can you predict a dividend cut? Payout ratios, balance-sheet strength, and short-run prospects for profits are all important, but lack of an economic moat is an overarching factor that correlates with substantially higher risk to dividends. Table 5.2 shows the results of our 2011 study of the interplay between economic moat ratings and dividend cuts among the U.S. companies we cover. The chance of a no-moat company cutting its dividend in a one-year forward time horizon was twice that of a wide-moat company. (The cuts were slightly larger as well, but when the barber takes out the scissors, it's rarely for a trim.)

Thanks to a focus on both economic moats and above-average and growing dividends, *DividendInvestor*'s two model portfolios have outperformed the S&P 500 by a substantial margin over time, as shown in Figure 5.2. We don't outperform every year, and we don't expect to. Yet curiously—or perhaps not so curiously—our outperformance correlates closely with the higher yields we have earned from our holdings. On a price-only basis that excludes dividend income, our portfolio holdings have slightly underperformed the S&P. However, by collecting annual dividend yields averaging 2.9 percentage points higher than the S&P, our total returns have outperformed this key benchmark by 2.2 percentage points annually from our January 2005 inception through September 2013. Figure 5.3 demonstrates that a significantly higher proportion of our

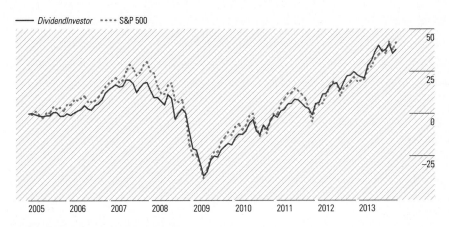

Figure 5.2 Cumulative Price Appreciation (%)
Data from Jan. 7, 2005, to Sept. 30, 2013.
SOURCE: Morningstar.

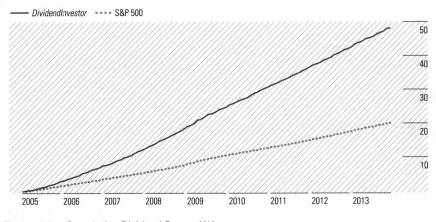

Figure 5.3 Cumulative Dividend Return (%)
Data from Jan. 7, 2005, to Sept. 30, 2013.
SOURCE: Morningstar.

performance comes from dividends, when compared with the S&P 500. Not only has our strategy outperformed the S&P, but the margin of outperformance has come directly from our above-average dividend yields, and we've experienced significantly less price volatility than the market as a whole.

In recent years, above-average dividend yields have been concentrated in several sectors including consumer staples, utilities, communications services, and midstream energy, where many companies have narrow and wide economic moats. Elsewhere in the U.S. equity market, dividend yields and payout ratios remain quite low by historic standards. The long-run average dividend yield of the S&P 500 is in the neighborhood of 4% with 50%–55% payout ratios; in 2013, payout ratios are running in the mid-30% range with a yield barely north of 2%. Over time, we expect shifting demographics—specifically a large increase in the number of retirees leaning on their portfolios for income—to drive increased payout ratios and yields in sectors where dividends have been downplayed or ignored for the past few decades. As that process unfolds, opportunities to earn generous yields will rise up in less-traditional fields.

The lesson here: If you're focused on income, we urge you to pay close attention to economic moats in your analysis. By itself, no dividend—regardless of size—can turn a bad business into a good long-term investment. But a dividend can turn a moat-protected, financially healthy business into a sound provider of income and total returns.

6

The Importance of Valuation

Contributed by Joel Bloomer, Matt Coffina, and Gareth James, members of Morningstar's Moat Committee and contributors to Morningstar's valuation methodology

So far we've talked about how to identify high-quality companies, including those with economic moats protecting their excess returns, those with improving competitive advantages, and those that are good stewards of capital. Now we explore how to value these businesses, and how to know when they are cheap or expensive.

When we talk about value we are referring specifically to intrinsic or fair value as opposed to share price. We agree with Warren Buffett's famous quote that "price is what you pay; value is what you get." Over the long term, we expect share prices to converge toward fair value, but in the short and medium term, stock markets can overreact and underreact to events, thereby creating investment opportunities. In such situations, a robust understanding of the underlying fair value of a business is imperative to making sound investment decisions and differentiates the investor from the speculator.

The intrinsic value of a business can be described as the present value of the excess cash generated during its remaining life. This methodology is commonly known as *discounted cash-flow*, or DCF, analysis, and the discount rate should reflect an adequate return on investors' capital. Of course, no one knows the exact intrinsic value of a business, but there are some tools we can employ to narrow the range of possible outcomes and identify the best opportunities. At Morningstar, we base our intrinsic or fair value estimates on detailed company, industry, and macroeconomic analysis combined with our consistent methodology framework and thorough peer review process.

To illustrate the power of this approach, Figure 6.1 shows the median price/fair value, or P/FV, chart for our entire coverage universe over the past decade. When stock prices rise above our fair value estimates, the P/FV is greater than 1, and we consider stocks to be overvalued at this level. Conversely, when share prices fall below our fair value estimates, the P/FV falls below 1, where we consider stocks to be undervalued. The chart shows how, in the optimism leading into the global financial crisis, our stock-specific fair values led us to be "fearful when others were greedy," following the dictum by Warren Buffett. In contrast, in the depths of the financial crisis we were "greedy when others were fearful," in keeping with Buffett's famous words. The fair value estimate is critical to this investment approach and to outperforming the market. Over time we expect share prices to converge to fair value, thereby enabling value to be realized. Estimating a company's fair value allows you to avoid some of the behavioral mistakes common in the market, such as overestimating the impact of a bad earnings report on a company's underlying business.

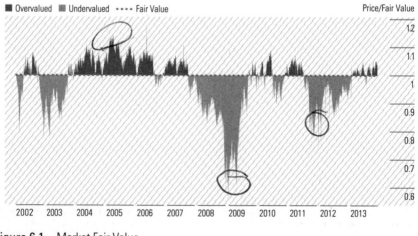

Figure 6.1   Market Fair Value
SOURCE: Morningstar.

Valuation Concepts

Before we explain how we use the DCF approach to establish the fair value of a stock, let's talk about valuation more generally. A common and simple valuation approach often used in the stock market is multiples-based analysis. In the same way that savers seek out high deposit rates, stock investors often look for high yields. One of the most commonly used approaches is the earnings yield— or, more accurately, its inverse, the price/earnings, or P/E, ratio. Other multiples such as price/sales, price/cash flow, and price/book value are also often used. The P/E valuation approach involves identifying a fair P/E multiple for a stock and then buying when the multiple is below this level and selling when the multiple is above it. This metric is relatively easy to calculate, requiring only the current share price and next year's earnings forecast, but there are many drawbacks to this and other multiples techniques.

Using multiples can be difficult if profits are expected to change significantly beyond the next financial year. Examples of businesses with big swings in profits include cyclical companies, high-growth companies, and assets with finite lives such as mines. There is also the problem of determining an appropriate multiple to use, and investors often look to similar companies and apply the same multiple across a peer group. Aside from the difficulty in finding sufficiently similar businesses, this technique risks a cycle of self-feeding overvaluation, as occurred during the technology stock bubble of the late 1990s. At Morningstar, we don't dismiss multiples altogether but rather use them as supporting cross-checks for our DCF-based fair value estimates. While we wouldn't use multiples to determine a company's fair value, it does make good sense to understand how the market is currently valuing a given company, and multiples can provide some insight into that value.

In contrast to the simplicity of multiples, discounted cash-flow analysis requires detailed forecasts of free cash flow that we discount to present value using a discount rate. Free cash flow is the money left over after all operating expenses and necessary investments in the business. This cash is available, or "free," to be distributed to investors (both shareholders and bondholders) through dividends, share repurchases, bond coupons, and debt principal repayment. Discounting is necessary because cash received in the future is worth less than cash on hand today, for two reasons: (1) if you had the cash today, you could invest it and earn interest, and (2) there's a chance something will happen that prevents you from receiving the cash in the future. The greater the risk of the cash not being received, the larger your discount rate should be—that is, the less cash you'd be willing to give up today in exchange for the future payment.

Cost of Capital and Returns on Capital

Put simply, the aim of investment is to generate risk-adjusted returns that exceed the cost of capital required to fund the investment. When evaluating returns generated by a business, we prefer to consider the underlying return by excluding nonoperating charges or income, and by excluding the benefits of financial leverage. To do this, we start with operating income (earnings before interest and taxes, or EBIT), then back out the effects of nonoperating charges or income and subtract cash taxes to arrive at earnings before interest, or EBI. That is our numerator, or the "return" part of the equation. To calculate the relevant capital invested in the business, we only consider capital that's required to generate profits. To exclude the benefits of financial leverage, we include invested capital from both equityholders and debtholders. Invested capital, or IC, is the denominator in our equation. This excludes assets owned by the business but not required to generate profits. We believe these metrics give the most realistic indication of investment return or return on invested capital, or ROIC. As we have discussed earlier, we often look for returns on invested capital and returns on new invested capital, or RONIC, to exceed a company's weighted average cost of capital, or WACC, as quantitative evidence of a moat. When we talk about returns we therefore mean:

$$\text{ROIC} = \frac{\text{EBI}}{\text{IC}}$$

Sometimes we include various other balance-sheet items, such as deferred tax assets, net liabilities, goodwill, or other intangibles, in the invested capital figure. Other adjustments can also improve the comparability and usefulness of ROIC; for example, some analysts choose to capitalize research and development or lease expenses to get a more accurate measure of invested capital. RONIC is similar to ROIC, except that it focuses exclusively on incremental earnings generated by incremental investment. A company may be earning high returns on legacy assets, but may lack the ability to invest new capital at a high rate of return. Both ROIC and RONIC can be compared against the weighted average cost of capital to determine whether a company is generating excess returns.

As all businesses require capital to operate, the cost of capital must be overcome in order to generate excess returns. We determine a WACC that incorporates the cost of both debt and equity, with weights of each dependent on the expected capital structure of the business. The WACC, which is also used as the discount rate in a discounted cash-flow model, incorporates the return required by both stockholders (the cost of equity, or COE) and bondholders (the cost of debt, or COD).

Morningstar's Valuation Approach

At Morningstar, we build DCF models for each of the companies in our coverage universe using a standard template. In practice, most DCF models have detailed cash-flow forecasts for five to 10 years, with this period typically referred to as the *explicit forecast period*. Beyond this, there is often little value in continuing detailed cash-flow forecasts as accuracy diminishes. As an alternative, some form of lump sum is generally used, typically referred to as the *perpetuity* or *terminal* value, and based on the final year's cash-flow forecast contained in the explicit period. To calculate a reasonable terminal value, it is important to reach a midcycle cash-flow forecast by the end of the explicit forecast. This type of model can be referred to as a two-stage DCF.

At Morningstar, we use a modified version of the traditional DCF, with explicit ties to our economic moat research and methodology. Our fundamental thesis is that for all firms, excess returns or economic profits will eventually be eroded by competition, but that this process will take significantly longer when the business possesses an economic moat to protect those excess returns.

From a modeling perspective, we incorporate our moat methodology into our financial models by expanding the traditional DCF to three stages as illustrated in Figure 6.2. We retain the detailed cash-flow period or explicit forecast period, which we refer to as Stage 1. However, we then incorporate a second stage during which we assume any excess returns are eroded by competition. Finally, by Stage 3 we assume excess returns have been eroded and RONIC = WACC. For companies with no economic moat, excess returns will be eroded quickly and Stage 2 will be short. But for companies with an economic moat, excess returns will be sustained for at least 10 years if the moat is narrow, or at least 20 years if the moat is wide. The length of Stage 2 is therefore dependent on the competitive advantage the company holds.

To incorporate a three-stage approach to calculate the fair value estimate, we simply sum the present values of the three stages, deduct the value of net debt, and divide by the number of shares on issue. After the Stage 1 explicit forecast period, Stage 2 in our model assumes that EBI grows at a fixed rate and that the company needs to reinvest a proportion of annual EBI to grow. These assumptions act as a proxy for explicit forecasts, as discussed earlier. In Stage 3, we capitalize EBI at the cost of capital and use this terminal value as a proxy for cash flows into perpetuity. From a returns perspective, the picture is often akin to Figure 6.3, where RONIC exceeds WACC in Stage 1, fades toward WACC in Stage 2, and is equal to WACC in Stage 3.

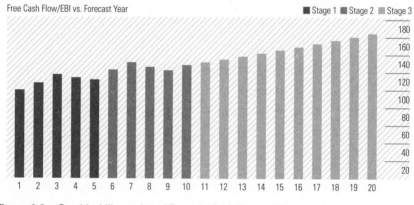

Figure 6.2   Graphical Illustration of Example Cash-Flow Profile
Source: Morningstar.

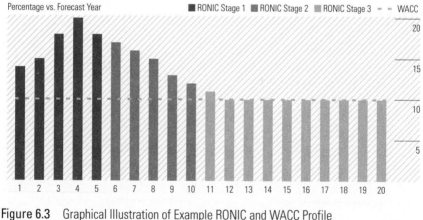

Figure 6.3   Graphical Illustration of Example RONIC and WACC Profile
Source: Morningstar.

Example: Calculating ROIC

To illustrate the calculation of ROIC, let's use a company Morningstar considers to have a wide economic moat: Patterson, a distributor of dental, veterinary, and medical supplies. Patterson's wide moat is based on a cost advantage—the company is one of only a few national dental and animal health distributors with the scale to effectively leverage investments in warehouses, logistics networks, and customer and supplier relationships. Table 6.1 displays Patterson's balance sheet for fiscal 2012 and 2013 (Patterson's fiscal year ends in April).

We can use the balance sheet to calculate Patterson's invested capital. For the purposes of this exercise, let's make the simplifying assumption that all of Patterson's cash and equivalents are necessary to operations and that goodwill, other long-term assets, other long-term liabilities, and deferred income taxes

Table 6.1 Patterson's Balance Sheet (Values in $ Millions)

	April 2012	April 2013
Cash and Equivalents	574	505
Receivables	465	448
Inventory	320	361
Prepaid Expense and Other	45	47
Total Current Assets	1,404	1,361
Property and Equipment	196	192
Long-Term Receivables	92	85
Goodwill	810	824
Identifiable Intangibles	213	197
Other	26	23
Total Assets	2,740	2,682
Accounts Payable	208	250
Accrued Payroll Expense	66	71
Other Accrued Expense	130	128
Current Maturities of Long-Term Debt	125	0
Total Current Liabilities	530	449
Long-Term Debt	725	725
Deferred Income Taxes	82	93
Other	28	21
Total Liabilities	1,364	1,287
Total Stockholders' Equity	1,375	1,395

NOTE: Companies with preferred stock in their capital structure will have an additional term in the WACC formula.
SOURCE: Patterson annual report.

should not be included in invested capital because they're not being utilized in operations. Under these assumptions, Patterson's invested capital at the end of fiscal 2012 and 2013 is calculated in Table 6.2.

Table 6.3 displays Patterson's income statement for fiscal 2011–13. We can use the income statement to calculate Patterson's earnings before interest.

Table 6.2 Patterson's Invested Capital (Values in $ Millions)

	April 2012	April 2013
Cash and Equivalents	574	505
Receivables	465	448
Inventory	320	361
Prepaid Expense and Other	45	47
Property and Equipment	196	192
Long-Term Receivables	92	85
Identifiable Intangibles	213	197
Operating Assets	1,904	1,836
Accounts Payable	208	250
Accrued Payroll Expense	66	71
Other Accrued Expense	130	128
Operating Liabilities	405	449
Invested Capital (Op. Assets—Op. Liabilities)	1,499	1,387

Source: Patterson annual report.

Table 6.3 Patterson's Income Statement (Values in $ Millions)

	April 2011	April 2012	April 2013
Net Sales	3,416	3,536	3,637
Cost of Sales	2,271	2,373	2,446
Gross Profit	1,144	1,163	1,191
Gross Margin %	33.5	32.9	32.7
Operating Expenses	768	805	836
Operating Income	376	358	355
Operating Margin %	11.0	10.1	9.7
Other Income, Net	6	2	3
Interest Expense	−26	−30	−36
Pretax Income	356	330	321
Income Taxes	131	117	111
Effective Tax Rate %	36.7	35.5	34.5
Net Income	226	213	210
Diluted Shares Outstanding	119	111	104
Diluted Earnings Per Share	1.89	1.92	2.03

Source: Patterson annual report.

The simplest calculation of EBI is to take net income plus tax-affected interest expense. In this case, for 2013,

$$EBI = 210 + 36 \times (1 - 34.5\%) \approx 234$$

To calculate ROIC, we normally use an average of the previous year's and current year's invested capital ($1,443 million for Patterson in 2012–13). Return on invested capital is thus as:

$$ROIC = EBI/\text{Average invested capital}$$
$$ROIC = 234/1,443 \approx 16.2\%$$

Next, let's calculate Patterson's weighted average cost of capital. Investors should normally use the market value of debt and equity to determine the weightings of each, but for the purposes of this example, we will use book values.

Patterson's total debt outstanding at the end of 2013 was $725 million. Shareholders' equity was $1,395 million. So total capital was $725 million + $1,395 million = $2,120 million. This is higher than our estimate of Patterson's invested capital because we assumed certain assets were nonoperating in nature, most importantly goodwill.

Patterson's capital-structure weighting toward equity is $1,395 million/$2,120 million $\approx 65.8\%$. The weighting toward debt is $725 million/$2,120 million $\approx 34.2\%$.

We also need an estimate of Patterson's cost of debt and cost of equity. Cost of debt can be calculated using observed interest expense. Patterson paid $36 million of interest expense in 2013, while average debt was $787.5 million (averaging total debt from the end of fiscal 2012 and 2013, including $125 million in short-term debt in 2012). Patterson's effective cost of debt can be estimated as:

$$COD = 36/787.5 \approx 4.6\%$$

The cost of equity presents considerably greater challenges, because it can't be observed in the real world. The cost of equity reflects the return expected by investors in a fairly valued stock. Morningstar uses a modified version of the capital asset pricing model, or CAPM, to assign cost-of-equity values, which range between 8% and 14% for companies in most developed markets under our methodology. For Patterson, we estimate the cost of equity at 10%, which is the most common value used across our coverage universe and reflects an average level of systematic risk (also called *market risk*, or the kind of risk that can't be reduced through diversification).

Plugging the values derived earlier into the formula for WACC, we estimate Patterson's cost of capital as:

$$WACC = w_d \cdot COD \cdot (1 - \textit{Tax rate}) + w_e \cdot COE$$
$$WACC = 34.2\% \cdot 4.6\% \cdot (1 - 34.5\%) + 65.8\% \cdot 10\%$$
$$WACC \approx 7.6\%$$

Because Patterson's ROIC of 16.2% exceeds its WACC of 7.6%, the company is earning excess returns on capital. Excess returns on capital indicate that an economic moat may be present, although these excess returns on their own are not sufficient evidence of a moat (we must also assess Patterson's qualitative characteristics to determine that the company has a sustainable competitive advantage).

Note that the adjustments you choose can have a significant impact on this analysis. For example, if we had included average goodwill of $817 million in Patterson's invested capital, this would have reduced ROIC to 10.4% (though this is still comfortably above Patterson's estimated cost of capital).

Forecasting Future Free Cash Flows

The most challenging aspect of estimating a company's fair value is predicting future cash flows. Experienced investors know that finding investing opportunities boils down to having a better forecast for future cash flows than the market does. All of the favorite theoretical arguments about discount rate and terminal value methodologies fade into the background, and what matters most is having better foresight about a company's future profits and cash flows than other investors do. Moreover, because the final year of the explicit forecast period is the basis for terminal value in any DCF methodology—not just Morningstar's—forecasting "normal" or "midcycle" earnings and cash flows is of utmost importance. Therefore, this is where we spend quite a bit of time. And we believe the focus on long-term competitive dynamics that underpins our moat and trend ratings also supports our valuation work by prioritizing our research efforts where they're needed most—on determining the longer-term earnings and cash-flow generation capabilities of a company.

Getting from EBI to free cash flow is relatively straightforward. You merely subtract net new investment—which includes capital expenditures, net investment in working capital (inventory, receivables, and payables), and acquisitions, less depreciation and divestitures. We distinguish between free cash flow to the firm (which belongs to both shareholders and bondholders) and free cash flow to equity (which is what's left for shareholders after paying all obligations to creditors). We use free cash flow to the firm because we are estimating the value of the entire enterprise, not just the value of the cash left for equityholders.

Although historical free cash flow can be readily calculated from the financial statements, projecting future results is a different matter. Key assumptions include future revenue growth, normalized operating margins, and net investment in working capital and property, plant, and equipment. Although historical results provide a starting point, there's no guarantee that the future will look like the past. The market often extrapolates recent performance, so some of the most valuable investment insights are gained when you can identify ahead of time that a company is at an inflection point, with results poised to either improve or deteriorate.

To help make good predictions about the future, analysts will normally break down key financial-statement line items into their component parts. For example, revenue growth and margins may differ by geography, segment, or product line. By making forecasts at a more granular level than the consolidated financial statements, you can improve your understanding of the drivers of performance. We consider numerous factors when making projections, such as (1) the company's competitive position, (2) industry dynamics and growth, (3) management's strategy and ability to execute, (4) the bargaining power of customers and suppliers, and (5) external factors such as regulation, the economy, technological developments, and demographic and social trends.

Economic moats have a direct influence on cash-flow forecasts. Companies with strong competitive advantages usually exhibit some combination of higher free cash flow relative to earnings (because of lower reinvestment requirements), faster growth (because capital that is reinvested has a high incremental earnings contribution), or both. On the other hand, exceptional growth and

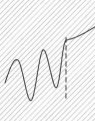

| Incorrect: Trough earnings used as jumping-off point for Stages 2–3 | Incorrect: Peak earnings used as jumping-off point for Stages 2–3 | Correct: Midcycle earnings used as jumping-off point for Stages 2–3 |

Figure 6.4   Choosing an EBI Forecast in the Last Year of Stage 1
SOURCE: Morningstar.

profitability won't go unnoticed by the competition, and firms that lack economic moats may experience market-share losses, pricing pressure, margin contraction, or falling returns on capital.

One of the most important assumptions in a valuation model is EBI in the last year of the explicit forecast period. Since Morningstar's analysts make specific projections for the first five to 10 years of their models (Stage 1), the last year of Stage 1 serves as the jumping-off point for all future years. Earnings in this year must be reflective of a normalized, midcycle level of both revenue and margins. If Stage 1 ends with earnings at a cyclical peak or otherwise unsustainable environment, the fair value estimate is certain to be too high. Similarly, if Stage 1 ends with earnings at a cyclical trough, you will inevitably underestimate intrinsic value. This idea is illustrated in Figure 6.4.

Estimating the intrinsic value of a common stock is really more art than science. There are many, many assumptions involved in a discounted cash-flow model. The future is inherently unpredictable, and no matter how much research and analysis we do, unexpected things will happen: technological advancements, shifting consumer preferences, regulatory or legal actions, emergence of new competitors, and so on. Pros and cons of DCF analysis are shown in Table 6.4.

One of the best tools for coping with future uncertainty is scenario analysis. Morningstar's analysts don't just make a single point estimate of a company's

Table 6.4   Pros and Cons of Discounted Cash-Flow Analysis

Pros	Cons
DCF valuation is extremely flexible; it allows you to account for almost any circumstance imaginable.	The future is inherently unpredictable; the further out in time you project results, the more likely you are to be wrong.
DCF enables you to incorporate multiple years of forecasts and can be used on companies with losses or unusually rapid growth in the near term.	A DCF-based valuation is only as good as the inputs; the "garbage in, garbage out" rule applies.
The most common alternative—applying a price/earnings multiple to a single year's earnings—is overly short-term-focused and requires the choice of an appropriate P/E multiple, which is often arbitrary.	Free cash flow is not the same thing as dividends. Management may end up squandering cash on bad investments or destroying shareholder value by letting cash accumulate on the balance sheet, earning a subpar return.
You don't have to be exactly right, as long as you invest with a margin of safety (that is, buy stocks only when they are trading at a discount to your best estimate of intrinsic value).	

Source: Morningstar.

fair value. Rather, we always consider at least three scenarios: a base case, a bull case, and a bear case. In the bull case, we believe there is a 25% probability that the company will exceed our optimistic assumptions. Likewise, our bear case assumes a 25% probability that the company will underperform our pessimistic predictions. We try to stay focused on the fact that there are a range of possibilities for a company's intrinsic value—if pinning down a precise appraisal were easy, stocks would always be fairly valued and this whole exercise would be a waste of time.

If a company faces a symmetric set of potential future outcomes, we might envision its fair value as being represented by a probability bell curve, as in Figure 6.5.

Many factors influence a company's valuation, but one of the most important is the presence of an economic moat. A strong competitive advantage enables a firm to invest capital at an attractive rate of return, so that growth translates to shareholder value creation. Without a moat, a company risks seeing any excess returns eroded by the competition.

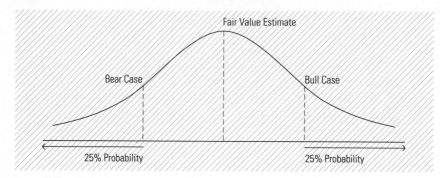

Figure 6.5   Scenario Analysis
Source: Morningstar.

The Morningstar Rating™ for Stocks

Next let's explore how we move from these fair value estimates to the Morningstar Rating™ for stocks, which essentially summarizes our view on a stock's investment attractiveness given the current stock price, our fair value estimate, and our level of uncertainty. We define our ratings so you understand exactly how we intend for them to be used (and how we use them ourselves). Figure 6.6 conveys where we are in the research process—the home stretch.

If you've worked with DCF models before, you know they can be highly sensitive and subjective tools. Even the most well-intentioned analyst can, after months or even years of work, miss the mark on a company's intrinsic value despite what seems like a reasonable set of assumptions. We'd like to think we're better than average at developing best practices, methodologies, and quality control measures to ensure that the assumptions driving our valuations are accurate. Still, it's an imprecise science, which brings us to another key piece of our methodology that we haven't discussed much yet—our confidence in each fair value estimate, codified in our valuation Uncertainty Ratings. The combination of our fair value estimate and our uncertainty rating on any given company leads us to the Morningstar Rating™ for stocks.[1] To illustrate the uncertainty rating and the role it plays in our system, let's briefly define the star rating: It's essentially a forward-looking, uncertainty-adjusted investment rating indicating the likely direction and magnitude of a stock's future returns.

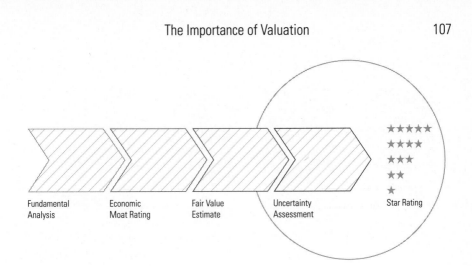

| Fundamental
Analysis | Economic
Moat Rating | Fair Value
Estimate | Uncertainty
Assessment | Star Rating |

Figure 6.6   The Morningstar Rating™ for Stocks
SOURCE: Morningstar.

Fair Value Uncertainty and Cost of Equity

So what exactly do we mean by uncertainty? We're basically asking, "How likely is it that I'm wrong in my estimates of the intrinsic value of the security I'm analyzing?" Our approach, after more than a decade of iteration and research, is to use five buckets of uncertainty: low, medium, high, very high, and extreme, each with a corresponding margin of safety. Every company that we cover receives an uncertainty rating, and we require a specified margin of safety around our fair value estimate before we'll pound the table on a buying opportunity and rate it 5 stars. A 1-star rating indicates that we think a company is significantly overvalued and we'd consider selling it if we happened to own it. As you might expect, the margin of safety we require increases as valuation predictability decreases. Put another way, as valuation uncertainty increases, so does the prudent margin of safety. Figure 6.7 demonstrates our system.

For situations where our uncertainty is low, meaning our confidence in forecasting the possible outcomes is relatively high, a 5-star rating is triggered when the stock trades at a 20% discount to fair value. If our uncertainty is very high, on the other hand, we require a 50% discount to fair value to award 5 stars. In between, if uncertainty is medium, the required discount is 30%, and for high uncertainty, it's 40%. So, for example, if we've determined that a reasonable base-case fair value estimate for a stock is $20 per share, we'd

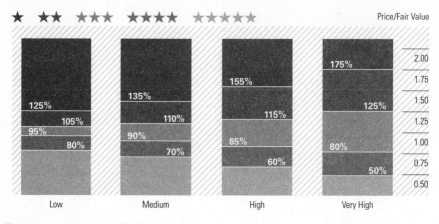

Figure 6.7   Uncertainty Rating
Source: Morningstar.

Table 6.5   Valuation Uncertainty Rating

Systematic Risk	+	Nonsystematic/Company-Specific Risk
Cost of equity		All non-COE model assumptions
Revenue beta to economy		Regulatory changes
Operating leverage		Large license, contract, or patent expirations
Financial leverage		Highly concentrated customer base
		Changing competition
		Risk of disruption or disintermediation
		Price taker in a volatile market
		Unpredictable management
		Questionable capital allocation

Source: Morningstar analysis.

consider buying at $16 with a low uncertainty rating, $14 with medium uncertainty, $12 with high uncertainty, and $10 with very high uncertainty. We use the extreme uncertainty rating to capture situations where we believe the margin of safety required is infinite. We still develop an "indicative" fair value in these cases, but we generally believe an investment would just be too risky, as there are surely greener pastures.

When establishing our uncertainty ratings, we divide risk into two buckets: systematic and nonsystematic (or company specific). Our uncertainty rating takes both of these into account, as Table 6.5 demonstrates. Essentially, when choosing an uncertainty rating we try to consider any factor that could affect valuation.

In our framework, we measure systematic risk as a company's beta, or sensitivity, to the economy—for any given change in GDP, how much does the relevant company's intrinsic value change? This is sometimes called *nondiversifiable risk*. As a reminder, we account for this nondiversifiable, systematic risk in our cost-of-equity assumption.

Nonsystematic, company-specific risk encompasses all remaining valuation influences. Examples include potentially material regulatory changes; large license, contract, or patent expirations; a highly concentrated customer base; rapidly changing competition; positioning as a price taker in a volatile market; unpredictable management, particularly where strategy is in flux; and any other company-specific factor that is difficult to predict but may have a material impact on our intrinsic value estimate. The more material the uncertainties are, the higher our uncertainty rating. Conversely, fewer unpredictable forces lead to a lower uncertainty rating.

In sum, the uncertainty rating captures anything—systematic or nonsystematic—that might cause our intrinsic valuation to be inaccurate. After all of our detailed, pound-the-pavement research is complete, we step back and ask, "How close are we likely to be with our fair value estimate?"

Another method we use to answer the question of uncertainty is extensive scenario analysis, which we touched on briefly before. What if a recession were to occur next year? What if it were not just a recession but a debt crisis? What if that drug in development eventually reaches pharmacy shelves? Could war cause oil prices to skyrocket? What if online retail sales reach 50% market share? The possibilities to consider are endless, but for each company and each industry, there are usually a few key themes that deserve consideration from both bullish and bearish perspectives. With casinos, for example, we want to know whether their licenses are exclusive, when they expire, how material each license is, and how likely they are to renew. For banks, we want to know whether their lending standards are aggressive, where bombs could be hiding on the balance sheet, how large an equity cushion they have to absorb the unexpected. For natural-resources companies, which are almost always price takers, we want to know how well they can absorb price declines and what operating leverage they may see on the upside if an unexpected supply squeeze occurs.

As our analysts consider various scenarios, it starts to become clear that there is a reasonable range for a particular fair value estimate. A good analyst, when asked about his or her estimated fair value for a company, will often respond with something like, "Probably about $20, but almost certainly between $16 and $25." As we willingly consider outcomes that could be materially different than our base-case assumptions but are nonetheless feasible, confidence intervals begin to appear and inform our uncertainty ratings, and thus our buy-and-sell recommendations. A stock price of $16 is a 20% discount to a $20 fair value estimate, and $25 is a 25% premium, which matches well with our medium uncertainty rating. Or if the "comfortable" range after scenario analysis were between $10 and $35, a very high uncertainty rating would be the better fit. More on the development of these bands in a moment.

There's a relative, common-sense element to choosing uncertainty ratings, too. Take, for example, Coca-Cola, American Express, Amazon.com, First Solar, and National Bank of Greece. As you can probably guess, this list represents increasing valuation uncertainty. How much is Coke consumption affected by politics, oil prices, regulation, and all the other vagaries that most companies must contemplate to accurately forecast demand for their products? The answer is, not much. Compare that with National Bank of Greece: It's hard to know what the next decade holds for the country as a whole let alone for an institution that is financially leveraged to it. American Express is an outstanding company but a bit more exposed than Coca-Cola to capital markets and fluctuations in consumer spending. Amazon.com is an amazing company but it faces a lot of competition and regularly reinvests most of what it earns—sometimes to scale up and sometimes to offer completely new services that aren't necessarily proven, bringing uncertainty. First Solar is a decent operator but is wholly dependent on government subsidy; its future is very uncertain and industry capacity has skyrocketed, led in part by central planning in China, causing supply to jump and prices to plummet.

So now that we've touched on risk and uncertainty, what's the difference between the two? If you look up "risk" in a general dictionary, the definition will likely focus primarily on the chance of loss but won't have much to say about unexpected upside. (Financial dictionaries are a little better about defining risk in terms of both potential upside and downside.) Look up "uncertainty," on the other hand, and the definition is likely to be more balanced, suggesting that things could turn out well or poorly, often without a bias toward one outcome or the other. So while there may not be much technical difference between risk and uncertainty, the connotation of risk is clearly biased to the downside, whereas uncertainty encompasses both upside and downside.

This idea of uncertainty on both the upside and downside plays out in our margin-of-safety categories. You may have noticed that as our uncertainty increases (meaning our confidence weakens), our 1-star trigger price moves farther away from our fair value estimates. For low uncertainty, a 1-star rating is triggered at a 25% premium to fair value; for medium, 35%; for high, 55%; and for very high, 75%. If we've determined that a sensible base-case fair value estimate is $20 per share, then for a low-uncertainty company, we'd consider selling at $25, and for a very-high-uncertainty company, $35. From a "risk" perspective, this approach can seem counterintuitive, but using an "uncertainty" lens, meaning our fair value estimate can be either high or low of the mark, the trigger points become logical. We want a larger margin of error around our estimate, so these trigger points widen out. Another way to think about this is that the area between our 5-star price and our fair value estimate is downside risk in the sense that the real intrinsic value could be less than our estimate. Conversely, the area between our fair value estimate and 1-star price is the upside potential, indicating that the future could be brighter than our forecasts. These ranges should be supported by scenario analysis for each company.

In summary, discounted cash-flow analysis can be a great tool for estimating the intrinsic value of a company. Looking at the range of possible outcomes for a given firm's cash flow and fair value helps round out the picture, and can help us estimate the margin of safety we'd like to see before investing. Of course, many factors influence a company's valuation, but the presence of an economic moat is of critical importance because a strong competitive advantage enables a firm to invest capital at an attractive rate of return.

Notes

1. For those familiar with the Morningstar Rating™ for funds, you can see that the Morningstar Rating™ for stocks differs in that our stock ratings reflect our prediction for future returns, while our fund ratings are based on historical performance compared to similar funds.

7

Do Moat Ratings Predict Stock Returns?

Contributed by Warren Miller, head of quantitative research at Morningstar

Analyzing competitive strengths and weaknesses can undoubtedly help management teams make better strategic decisions, but can this type of research also help investors make better choices and achieve better outcomes? In other words, is it worth precious time to dive deep into the intricacies of the moat framework? In this chapter, we use some simple statistical analysis to examine what our moat ratings can tell us about stock returns. We launched these ratings in 2002, which gives us more than a decade's worth of data to analyze. Of course, the following studies show how the moat ratings have performed in the past, and as always, there is no guarantee this performance will continue into the future.

Through our research, we've found that wide-moat stocks exhibit less downside risk and less upside potential. In times of market fear or distress, wide-moat stocks outperform no-moat stocks, but then underperform when risk aversion subsides. The evidence isn't quite strong enough to claim that all wide-moat stocks generate excess risk-adjusted returns, but we do find that undervalued wide-moat stocks have done so. We think it's safe to say, then, that the moat rating is a valuable risk-management and security-selection tool, especially when used in conjunction with valuation-based metrics.

The most direct way to look at the performance of moat ratings is to segment companies based on their moat ratings and examine the distribution of returns for each group subsequent to the date it received its moat rating.

Table 7.1 shows how stocks from each moat-rating group can be expected to perform over a one-month time horizon. Of course one month is very short to a long-term investor, but it's useful to study returns on this horizon for two reasons. First, there is a direct mathematical relationship between short-term returns and long-term returns: Long-term returns are the geometric mean of the short-term returns that compose the same period. Here, we are averaging monthly returns over more than a decade, giving us many datapoints over varying market conditions. Second, it is reasonable to assume that even a long-term investor may revisit portfolio constitution at a monthly frequency given the fluctuations in expected returns that happen over periods as short as one month.

The first thing we notice from Table 7.1 is that there is no differentiation in the mean one-month return across moat ratings. This means that if you were to choose one stock randomly from each of the three buckets and hold them for one month, you could expect each to earn the same return percentage over that one-month time period.

Of course, the mean tells us nothing about the risk involved in making these three investments. The standard deviation describes the dispersion of the return distribution, or how far away from that mean you might land. No-moat stocks have nearly double the standard deviation of wide-moat stocks, meaning

Table 7.1   Summary Statistics for Marginal Distributions of Future Monthly Returns by Moat Rating

	Wide	Narrow	None
Mean (%)	1.0	1.0	1.0
Standard Deviation (%)	6.9	8.7	13.2
Interquartile Range (%)	7.3	8.7	12.3
5th Percentile (%)	−9.6	−12.5	−18.9
Median (%)	0.7	0.8	0.5
95th Percentile (%)	11.5	14.3	20.8
Skew	0.0	0.3	1.2
Kurtosis	5.5	9.1	16.2

SOURCE: Morningstar.

there is a greater chance of landing far away from the mean return. This is also reflected in the larger interquartile range for no-moat stocks as compared with wide-moat stocks.

However, we find that the distributions are not symmetrical around the mean. In general, you want distributions where the upside potential is larger than the downside potential (also known as having a *positive skewness*). We see that no-moat stocks have the largest skewness, so the variation from the mean return is more likely to be a positive variation for no-moat stocks than for wide-moat stocks. This makes sense from an economic perspective given that wide-moat stocks tend to be more mature businesses that are much less likely to have explosive growth rates, while nearly every business, no matter the size or maturity, can be susceptible to large economic downturns, as we saw in the most recent financial crisis.

Finally, let's take a look at the tails of the distribution. The "fatness" of a distribution's tails, also referred to as *kurtosis*, tells us the likelihood of extremely positive or negative events. Based on the relatively high kurtosis of 16.2 for no-moat stocks, we know that extreme events happened far more frequently here than for wide-moat stocks.

So where does that leave us? We can conclude that no-moat stocks have behaved more extremely with far more dispersion from the mean than wide-moat stocks, while delivering no additional expected return. No-moat stocks do benefit from positive skewness given their greater potential for high growth, but overall, the risk/reward profile for the no-moat group has not been very attractive.

Table 7.1 doesn't tell the whole story. It ignores one very important dimension—time. By examining how stocks in each moat group behave over time, we can develop a sense for the consistency of the statistics in Table 7.1 and how wildly they can vary in different economic conditions.

Figure 7.1 shows us how portfolios based on the moat ratings would have performed since we started assigning ratings. As we saw in Table 7.1, we note again here that wide-moat stocks have less volatility and milder drawdowns than narrow- or no-moat stocks, but lower cumulative returns. By equalizing the risk characteristics of the three groups, we can judge the cumulative returns on a more apples-to-apples, or risk-adjusted, basis.

Indeed, if we adjust the narrow-moat and no-moat portfolios to match the volatility of the wide-moat portfolio, we can see that the no-moat portfolio

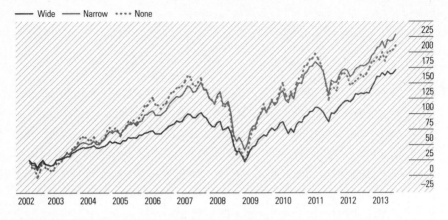

Figure 7.1 Cumulative Total Return of Moat Portfolios Rebalanced Monthly to Equal Weights (%)
SOURCE: Morningstar.

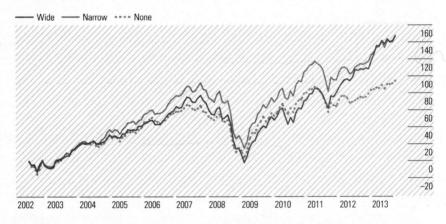

Figure 7.2 Cumulative Total Return of Volatility-Matched Moat Portfolios Rebalanced Monthly to Equal Weights (%)
SOURCE: Morningstar.

trails significantly behind its narrow- and wide-moat counterparts, as shown in Figure 7.2. Still, the payoff to being in wide-moat stocks has not been constant, and we see that wide-moat stocks don't outperform on a risk-adjusted basis over all time periods. This becomes clearer when we look at the rolling premium earned by the wide-moat portfolio relative to the no-moat portfolio over time.

Figure 7.3 shows that the premium of the wide-moat portfolio over the no-moat portfolio vacillates from positive to negative territory quite frequently. However, there is a clear departure from this behavior entering the financial

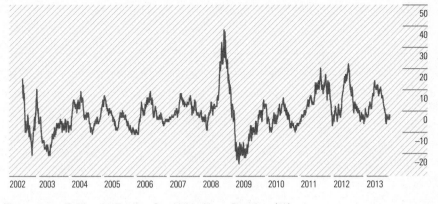

Figure 7.3 Rolling 90-Trading-Day Wide-None Premium (%)
SOURCE: Morningstar.

crisis in 2008. As the crisis became worse, the premium of wide moats over no moats became exaggerated to the positive side. This makes intuitive sense given the general increase in risk aversion during that time period. Conversely, the premium became significantly negative as the crisis subsided and risk aversion decreased. Monitoring the level and trend of this premium can be a solid indication of general market appetite for risk.

Despite the evidence provided earlier, we don't believe simply investing in wide-moat stocks is enough to ensure superior risk-adjusted returns in the long run. A stock's valuation, or its price relative to its intrinsic cash-flow-based valuation, is another major component to consider.

As we discussed in Chapter 6, we use a discounted cash-flow methodology to assign a fair value estimate to each stock we cover. By comparing that fair value estimate with the current price of the stock, you can immediately gauge our opinion on whether a given stock is over- or undervalued at any point in time. Undervalued stocks should be expected to earn positive risk-adjusted returns, and overvalued stocks should be expected to earn negative risk-adjusted returns.

One interesting phenomenon that we find with our rating methodology is that the accuracy of our valuations seems to vary by moat rating. On average, our valuations are more accurate when moats are wider. In Figure 7.4, you can see this in the much more orderly relationship between valuation decile and subsequent average returns for wide- and narrow-moat stocks than for no-moat stocks. In fact, the R-squared between valuation decile and subsequent returns

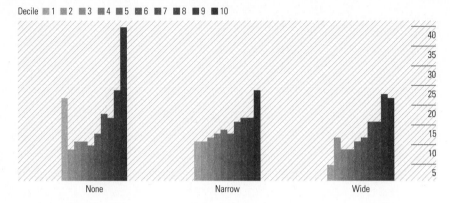

Figure 7.4 Annualized Daily Future Returns (%) by Moat Rating and Valuation Decile
Source: Morningstar.

among wide-moat stocks is 0.84—more than double the R-squared among no-moat stocks, which indicates high correlation between the valuation decile and the subsequent returns.

Why would this be the case? As we have discussed, stock prices of wide-moat companies are generally less volatile than their no-moat counterparts. If we think about stock price volatility as a proxy for earnings and cash-flow volatility of the underlying firm, we can conclude that wide-moat companies have less volatile cash flows than no-moat companies do. Given that we are attempting to forecast those cash flows, one might conclude that we can model wide-moat companies more reliably in a discounted cash-flow framework than more volatile no-moat firms.

All of the preceding studies tell us only about returns and risk in the context of individual securities. As investors we're also interested in how securities behave in portfolios. Once we combine individual securities into portfolios, we have the opportunity to diversify away the idiosyncratic risk inherent in picking individual stocks. The capital asset pricing model, or CAPM, can help us analyze our moat ratings in the portfolio context.

The CAPM is arguably the most well-known asset pricing model today. Like any model, it's a simplification of the world, and as such, its many flaws have been expounded on sufficiently in academic literature. A full treatment of the CAPM is outside the scope of this book. It suffices to say that the CAPM is a formula that describes an asset's expected future return in excess of the risk-free rate as proportional to the market's excess return. The exact proportion that equates these two excess returns is the stock's beta, a measure of its systematic or undiversifiable risk. The main tenet of the CAPM is that undiversifiable risk is the only risk for which an investor should be compensated because all other risk can, by definition, be diversified away in a portfolio.

In reality, of course, asset returns don't perfectly match the CAPM, so we include an error term in the equation to account for how far an asset's return deviates from the model prediction after the fact. The mean of this error term is known as *alpha*, and it represents the portion of the security's return that is unexplained by the excess market return factor. As a result, positive alpha is return that was not accompanied by proportionate systematic risk and is a desirable trait for an investment to have.

If markets were truly efficient, there would be no way to predict alpha in advance (assuming you're using the true model of systematic risk). Although we don't know the true model of systematic risk, we can use the CAPM as a lens to investigate whether moat ratings tell us anything about alpha before the fact.

Table 7.2 shows the same summary statistics as Table 7.1 with one key difference: Table 7.2 is the distribution of alpha segmented by moat rating, instead of return segmented by moat rating. This allows us to see how an investor would do if they perfectly hedged out all idiosyncratic, or unsystematic, risk.

The chart shows that wide-moat stocks have earned 20 basis points more alpha than no-moat stocks each month. They also have lower alpha standard deviation, smaller interquartile ranges, and less downside risk. Wide moats still have a lower skew and kurtosis than narrow- or no-moat alphas as well. So, it appears that wide-moat stocks, minus their disadvantage in skewness, are

Table 7.2 Summary Statistics for Marginal Distributions of Future Monthly Alpha by Moat Rating

	Wide	Narrow	None
Mean (%)	0.1	0.0	−0.1
Median (%)	0.0	0.0	−0.4
Standard Deviation (%)	6.7	8.0	12.1
Interquartile Range (%)	7.2	8.3	11.6
5th Percentile (%)	−10.1	−12.2	−17.9
95th Percentile (%)	10.3	12.4	18.3
Skew	0.1	0.5	1.3
Kurtosis	6.1	8.1	15.9

Source: Morningstar.

more attractive to hold in a portfolio context. One other note, not shown in the chart, is that wide-moat stocks also have a lower beta (0.8) on average than narrow-moat (0.9) or no-moat (1.1) stocks—another indication of lower risk for wide moats.

All investors have limited amounts of time to analyze investment opportunities. Is it worthwhile to spend some of this precious time analyzing competitive advantages? We believe the answer is a resounding yes. Although no set of performance studies can be truly comprehensive (there are always more ways to slice and dice the data), we've provided some of our most intuitive evidence to show that moat analysis can help control risk and, in combination with valuation, generate excess risk-adjusted returns.

Putting Moat and Valuation to Work

Portfolio Strategies

Now that we've walked through how we estimate a company's moat rating and fair value, we would like to share a few real-world examples of how to put these principles into action. We start with the Wide Moat Focus Index, as it represents the most systematic application of these methods.

Wide Moat Focus Index

This index reflects the ideas we have articulated so far in this book, that both quality and valuation matter in stock investing. Wide Moat Focus is a rules-based index that holds the 20 cheapest wide-moat stocks, as determined by Morningstar analysts' economic moat ratings and fair value estimates. Wide Moat Focus considers only moat ratings and valuation, without regard to moat trend, stewardship, or uncertainty. To construct the index, we begin with a pool of all U.S.-based and U.S.-traded stocks with wide moat ratings (excluding

American Depositary Receipts, American Depositary Shares, and limited partnerships). We then rank this universe of approximately 130 companies by ratio
of market price relative to fair value estimate and include the 20 securities trading at the largest discounts to fair value. The holdings are weighted equally,
and the index is reconstituted and rebalanced quarterly.

Since its inception on Sept. 30, 2002, through Sept. 30, 2013, the
Morningstar® Wide Moat Focus Index^{SM} has generated annualized returns of
15.9%, versus 8.8% for the S&P 500. (We actually created the index in 2007,
but based on moat ratings and fair value estimates assigned starting in 2002,
we are able to create hypothetical results going back to September 2002. For
2007 to the present, the results are based on the index's actual performance.)
As you can see in Table 8.1, the Wide Moat Focus Index has performed well
over a decade that has seen many market conditions, including commodity
booms, a major financial crisis, a deep recession, and a boom-bust cycle in the
housing markets. The Wide Moat Focus Index's strong performance through
several major market fluctuations suggests a robust ability to adapt to the
market and identify high-quality undervalued stocks.

This index has been licensed for the creation of two exchange-traded products: an exchange-traded fund under the ticker MOAT, and an exchange-traded
note under the ticker WMW. Because the portfolio construction process is
rules-based, the index has fairly high turnover—on the order of 120%–150%
per year. This occurs because a security trading at a 25% discount to our fair
value estimate can be replaced by one trading at a 25.5% discount when we
reconstitute the portfolio each quarter. We designed the index construction
process to be as hands-off as possible, so that our bottom-up work on economic moats and intrinsic values would flow into the portfolios without any

Table 8.1   Annual Performance of Wide Moat Focus Index

	02*	03	04	05	06	07	08	09	10	11	12	YTD**
Morningstar® Wide Moat Focus Index^{SM} (%)	15.0	36.2	27.8	4.7	17.7	−1.3	−19.6	49.7	8.6	6.6	24.5	22.5
S&P 500 Index (%)		8.4	28.7	10.9	4.9	15.8	5.5	−37.0	28.3	15.1	2.1	16.0	19.8

*Partial year: returns from Oct. 1, 2002.
**YTD: Sept. 30, 2013.
SOURCE: Morningstar.

top-down intervention that could call into question whether the portfolio's returns stemmed from our analysts' security-specific analysis or from managerial overrides.

Few rational portfolio managers would actually replace a security trading at a 25% discount to their estimate of value with one trading at a 25.5% discount. For one, the transaction costs could eat up some of the potential alpha. Also, estimates of value are just that—estimates. You could overcome this issue by either using this wide-moat-focus strategy in a qualified account where short-term capital gains taxes would not chip away at returns, or by modifying the portfolio construction process to require that new portfolio entrants overcome a certain hurdle before being added. For example, maybe you'd require that a new stock be at least 5% more underpriced than the security it would be replacing. We've performed some internal simulations using a hurdle rate like this to bring down turnover, and those studies suggest that getting turnover down to about 50% might cost 150 to 200 basis points in annual performance. So, the turnover issue is manageable, but it's certainly something to keep in mind.

Interestingly, the vast majority of this turnover comes from changes in valuation due to stock-price movements, rather than frequent changes in our moat ratings or fair value estimates. As Figure 8.1 shows, we see less than 10% annual turnover in our moat ratings.

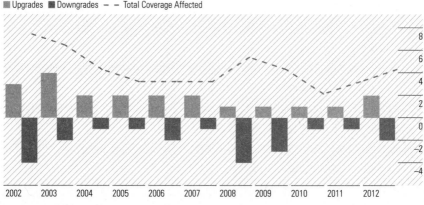

Figure 8.1 Moat Upgrades and Downgrades as a Percentage of Our Total Coverage Universe
Source: Morningstar estimates.

The Tortoise and Hare Portfolios

Another example of putting these principles into action comes from our *Morningstar® StockInvestor*[SM] newsletter. As part of this newsletter, we run two real-money portfolios, the Tortoise and the Hare, both of which have significantly outperformed the S&P 500 benchmark since their inception on June 18, 2001. For current performance figures, see http://msi.morningstar.com.

The Tortoise Portfolio includes our more conservative recommendations. These holdings tend to be mature, relatively slow-growing companies with moderate to low risk. All holdings have economic moats, with a strong bias toward companies with wide moats. We try to tilt the portfolio toward companies with stable or improving competitive advantages (stable or positive trend ratings). The Tortoise tends to lag a bit in strong bull markets, but more than make up for it in bear markets.

The Hare Portfolio includes our more aggressive picks. These companies tend to be faster-growing, with both higher risk and higher return potential than the firms in the Tortoise. All holdings have economic moats, though we're more willing to consider companies with narrow moats and positive moat trends in the Hare (that is, companies that are on their way toward building wide moats in the future). The Hare's performance has been more closely correlated with—though substantially better than—the overall market.

StockInvestor's Stock Selection Criteria

When picking stocks for the Tortoise and Hare Portfolios, we seek companies that:

- Possess sustainable competitive advantages, as measured by Morningstar's economic moat ratings.
- Have stable or improving competitive positions, as measured by Morningstar's moat trend ratings.
- Trade at discounts to their intrinsic values, as measured by Morningstar's price/fair value ratios.
- Trade with a margin of safety appropriate for the level of uncertainty underlying our fair value estimates, as measured by Morningstar's star ratings.
- Have management teams adept at strategic execution and capital allocation, as measured by Morningstar's stewardship ratings.

In other words, we consider all of the aspects of the research method-ology described throughout this book when choosing stocks for the Tortoise and Hare.

Portfolio Management Strategy

Picking good stocks is only part of what it takes to be a successful investor. Portfolio management strategy is also important, and at Morningstar, we follow a few key principles.

We view stocks as representing an ownership stake in a real business.

It seems like a basic point, but far too many people treat stocks as pieces of paper, and investing as a form of gambling. In fact, common stocks represent an ownership interest in a real business. Some portion of the cash flow generated by the businesses we own belongs to us, and we entrust management teams to use those cash flows wisely.

Thinking like an owner changes your whole perspective on stock investing. If a company has a bad quarter or two because it is making investments that will pay off in the future, that's a good thing. If a company's stock price falls when there's no change in fundamental outlook, that can be a good thing, too: It allows you to increase your ownership stake at a better price, either actively by buying more shares, or passively if the company is engaged in a share repurchase program.

We base decisions on reason and analysis, not emotion.

Investors can be their own worst enemies. It's easy to be optimistic when stock prices are rising, and just as easy to panic when prices fall. To be successful investors, we need to learn to suppress these natural instincts. To repeat one of Warren Buffett's most famous quotes, we need to "be fearful when others are greedy, and greedy when others are fearful."

There is no rule for whether to buy, sell, or hold when a stock goes either up or down. That's because, in isolation, stock-price movements tell you next to nothing. What really matters is how a stock's price compares with its intrinsic value. For example, say we estimate a company's intrinsic value at $100 per share, and the stock is trading for $80. Some news indicates that the company's long-run margins are likely to be much higher than we and other investors previously believed, and the stock appreciates 20% to $96 per share.

Is this stock more expensive at $96 than it was at $80? On the surface it may seem so, but the truth is we don't have enough information yet to know. That's like asking if a $500 stock is more expensive than a $50 stock—we need some reference to intrinsic value for stock prices to be meaningful (the $500 stock could undergo a 10:1 split and become a $50 stock tomorrow).

What if the higher long-run margin expectations boost our example company's fair value estimate by 30% to $130? In this case, the price/fair value ratio has decreased from 0.80 to 0.74—the stock is actually trading at a larger discount to fair value, implying better expected return prospects than before the news about margins. A similar principle applies when a stock falls—what matters is how the new price compares with the new intrinsic value, given all of the information available at the time. Without a grounding in intrinsic value, investing becomes little more than a game of chance.

If you can keep emotion out of your decisions, you'll have a significant advantage over the average individual investor. Part of keeping your emotions in check is having a realistic time horizon. It can take three years or longer for the market to recognize the value in a stock. Occasionally external events—like the 2008–09 global financial crisis—can temporarily make an undervalued stock much cheaper, even if the company's long-run cash flow outlook isn't materially altered by the event. Funds that will be needed in the next three to five years are much better off in cash or short-term bonds than in common stocks.

We maintain adequate diversification, without overdoing it.

A company's stock price depends on investors' current perceptions of the cash flows that the company can generate in the future. Of course, the future is inherently unpredictable. No matter how confident we are in our projections, there's always a risk that something unexpected will happen, causing a stock to be worth substantially more or less than we previously believed. Even when we can identify all of the risks and opportunities, and assign probabilities to them, there's no way to know exactly which future scenario will play out.

Because of this uncertainty, we attempt to keep the Tortoise and Hare diversified across industries and sectors, and most importantly to limit both portfolios' exposure to specific underlying risk factors and trends, such as commodity prices, interest rates, regulatory changes, the health of the housing market, increased adoption of smartphones, and so on. This way, if we're wrong about a prediction—say, oil prices end up lower than we forecast, or the housing market recovery is weaker than expected—the damage to the intrinsic value of our overall portfolios is limited.

Although diversification has clear benefits, it also has its disadvantages and limitations. The reduced volatility that comes with diversification drops off substantially as more securities are added to a portfolio. A portfolio with 20 stocks isn't that much more volatile than a portfolio with 40 stocks. More importantly, good investment opportunities are rare. If we insisted on holding a very large number of stocks, we would inevitably end up diluting our best ideas with mediocre picks. We target about 20 stocks each in the Tortoise and Hare.

We stay fully invested, most of the time.

In our view, there are only two ways to reliably beat the market. One is to buy stocks trading for less than fair value and wait until the market recognizes that value. The second is to buy shares in companies that are compounding their intrinsic values more quickly than average, usually because they have strong and growing competitive advantages. Ideally, we look for investment opportunities where we can benefit from both factors.

A much harder and less fruitful way to try to beat the market is to trade in and out of equities, attempting to time the highs and lows. We don't know of anyone who can do this with consistency. It's simply not possible to know ahead of time whether the market will rise or fall in any given day, week, month, or year. Moreover, stocks tend to increase in value over time, as the economy and corporate earnings grow. Over a long enough time horizon, the opportunity cost of not investing in stocks greatly outweighs the risks of staying invested through a bear market.

That said, there are advantages to maintaining a modest cash position. Having a little cash on hand enables you to take advantage of opportunities that may arise without having to sell something else to raise funds. Additionally, there are times when the market is so overvalued—such as the peak of the dot-com bubble—that it's impossible to find enough quality companies trading at reasonable prices to fill out a portfolio. In such circumstances, we prefer to hold cash and wait for better opportunities down the road. The rest of the time, we stay more or less fully invested.

> We trade infrequently.

The Tortoise and Hare have had very low turnover historically—averaging 17% per year between 2002 and 2012. That means our average holding period has been more than five years. Low turnover has a number of advantages, not least of which is the money you can save on taxes—both by paying at long-term instead of short-term capital-gains tax rates and by deferring taxes, with the money earning a return in the meantime. Low turnover also reduces trading costs such as commissions and bid-ask spreads. The average large-cap mutual fund has turnover of 75% per year, while generating worse performance than the Tortoise and Hare.

The desire to keep turnover low is a good reason not to shuffle money between companies with similar risk/reward profiles. However, it's not an excuse to hold onto a stock that is significantly overvalued or faces a deteriorating competitive position. If you think about it, at the end of the day, investors actually should seek to maximize their tax bills—by making very successful investments.

Summing Up

The Tortoise and Hare portfolios put Morningstar's research into action. We look for companies with wide moats, stable or improving competitive advantages, high-quality management teams, and decent margins of safety. We maintain diversified portfolios, think like business owners, and trade infrequently. The merits of our approach show in our track record of handily outperforming the S&P 500 over more than a decade, without taking on excessive risk.

9

Basic Materials

At this point in the book, we shift from general to specific and drill down into various sectors to see what drives moat creation for different types of companies. Think of the following chapters as a reference manual that you can refer back to when researching a particular company or sector. In each chapter, we provide an overview of that sector's moat landscape, discuss the factors that lead to wide and narrow moats for various industries, share some examples, and give you some key pointers to remember when doing your research. This is only the tip of the iceberg when it comes to the depth of our analysis around each sector, and we have chosen a small handful of industries in each sector to illustrate the key points. Our goal is to give you enough to get you started.

Let's start with basic materials. A glance at the periodic table of elements will give you a quick sense for the products that basic materials companies sell. If a company isn't directly producing one of the elements listed, chances are it's manufacturing a compound or alloy from a combination of elements.

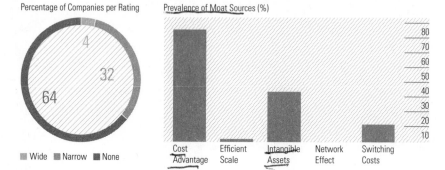

Figure 9.1   Economic Moat Characteristics in the Basic Materials Sector
Source: Morningstar.

By definition, basic materials companies deal in commodities, which isn't the most fertile territory for moat building. In commodity-based businesses, products are undifferentiated and prices are set by the law of supply and demand. These companies are considered price takers, meaning they have very little control over the prices of their products.

Given these dynamics, the key to gaining a competitive advantage and building a moat is the ability to produce commodities at lower cost than competitors. Ownership of world-class mineral deposits, access to low-cost feedstocks (for example, crude oil) and highly efficient production methods are the most common pathways to lower costs. Some companies have also created moats by building strong research and development, or R&D, pipelines or entwining themselves in their customers' businesses to create high switching costs. Unfortunately, though, many of these advantages are geologically finite or can eventually be replicated by competitors, so although some companies have secured enough of an advantage to establish narrow economic moats, wide moats are rare in the basic materials space, as Figure 9.1 shows.

Commodity Manufacturers

Commodity manufacturers—including companies that make steel, aluminum, and paper—produce intermediate or finished goods that serve as major components in end products such as infrastructure, buildings, automobiles, and household items. Using raw material that is mined, recycled, or harvested, these companies refine, smelt, or process to mass-produce essential components sold to original equipment manufacturers, or OEMs, builders, manufacturers, or end users.

A sustainable low-cost advantage is by far the main source of economic moat for commodity manufacturers. These firms produce undifferentiated commodities, so other potential moat sources—brands or patents, switching costs, network effect, and efficient scale–rarely come into play. Price is king for the commodity customer, so the ability to sustainably produce at a cost well below the prevailing price is really the only way to earn returns above the cost of capital. To keep operating costs in check, these firms must have access to cheaper raw materials and energy and use efficient, modern technologies in their production processes. It is not enough just to have a reliable supply of raw materials through ownership of raw material assets, though this might provide other benefits such as better working-capital management and quality control. The assets themselves must be low cost to be a moat source.

Wide economic moats require long-term confidence that is rare among commodity manufacturers. Raw materials from geological deposits eventually deplete, requiring manufacturers to continually hunt for new sources. In cases where the raw materials are renewable resources, the commodity nature of the end product makes it likely that the barriers to entry would be too low to prevent new competitors from entering the market, even if excess returns look sustainable for a 20-plus-year period.

These commodity manufacturers also have a few other factors working against them in their quest for moats. For example, all production equipment and processes require upgrades over time, allowing competitors to invest in similar low-cost facilities. Also, given government ownership in some commodity manufacturing as well as high operating leverage in some cases, there are often high-cost players that produce even when selling prices fall below the cost of production. Maximizing output rather than returns on capital can drive down economic profits for the whole industry, preventing lower-cost manufacturers from establishing wide moats.

Despite these inherent challenges, steel manufacturer Nucor has managed to establish a clear cost advantage and earn a narrow moat rating. Nucor's cost advantage stems, in large part, from its use of electric arc furnaces, or EAFs. Relative to blast furnaces, EAFs require a lower investment per unit of installed capacity and are significantly less energy- and labor-intensive.

Nucor is also managing costs by expanding its direct reduced iron, or DRI, production capacity. The use of DRI in steel production offers a variety of inroads to cost savings. First, because DRI does not need to melt, it can be processed at a lower temperature than feedstock consisting purely of scrap metal. This reduces electricity costs, which account for a significant portion of Nucor's cash cost of steel production. Because the DRI process occurs at lower temperatures, production equipment is also subject to less wear and tear, thereby allowing for lower maintenance and replacement costs. Additionally, because the natural gas steam used in the DRI production process contains fewer impurities than coal steam does, Nucor can produce stronger and higher-quality steel than peers that utilize pig iron. As a result, Nucor can manufacture a wide variety of steel products while other EAF producers typically offer a more limited product portfolio. Nucor's diverse portfolio reduces volatility associated with its revenue stream, providing us with a higher degree of confidence that the company will be able to consistently generate economic profits over the foreseeable future.

Nucor's transition to a DRI-based production process is still in its early stages, and before we could consider assigning a wide moat rating, we would need to see more concrete evidence that the firm's cost structure has improved materially. Since the financial crisis, Nucor has struggled to generate economic profit, and although we project that the company will be able to do so over the explicit forecast period, it's likely that the competition will be able to replicate Nucor's DRI-based production process within a 20-year period. Therefore, we believe a narrow moat rating is appropriate.

Key considerations for evaluating commodity manufacturers:

- Does the company have low production costs? Does the company have low capital costs? Look at the cost to build new capacity per unit. Depreciation, depletion, and amortization, or DD&A, costs per unit can be used as a proxy.
- Does the firm benefit from technology or geographic exposure that could be easily replicated?
- Does the firm have significant legacy costs or trouble managing its balance sheet? Although these will not typically affect the moat, they could reduce the company's financial flexibility and impair its ability to adequately invest in its business. Notice whether the company's capital expenditures are falling short, either relative to its depreciation expense or compared with its peers.

Commodity Processors

Commodity processors, such as chemicals companies and farm products firms, take inputs from natural resource extractors or other commodity processors and transform those inputs into outputs that serve as either building blocks or finished products in a variety of industries. Processors closer to natural-resource extractors in the value chain often produce basic building blocks, while processors further removed produce specialized products to exacting customer specifications.

Upstream commodity processors (those closest to natural resources in the value chain) generally make undifferentiated products. For example, a petrochemical producer that cracks ethane into ethylene is an upstream firm selling an undifferentiated commodity product. With these types of processing firms, as with commodity manufacturers, cost advantage is the principal moat source. But because commodity processors are often buying inputs in the open market instead of taking resources directly out of the ground, their cost advantages are not likely to be sustainable over the long term. That said, a handful of processors, such as BASF, control superior production processes that can lead to lasting cost advantages (more on BASF's competitive advantages below).

The situation is different for downstream processors, which produce more specialized products. Specialized products often carry higher margins, though they're not always sustainable over the long haul. Beware of products that sound specialized—or carry a specialty label from company management—but can be easily replicated by rivals. Patents can help provide protection from replication, and some processors have the advantage of controlling a portfolio of patented products (intangible assets) that can generate outsize returns during the life of the patent.

Specialty downstream processors can also benefit from customer switching costs. Some commodity processors have become deeply intertwined in their customers' processes, making it costly for the customers to switch to competing products. Some companies create switching costs via long-term on-site commodity contracts with customers that compensate buyers for the large up-front capital investment while helping establish a regional monopoly in the process. Still other processors benefit from efficient scale when potential new competitors are discouraged from entering relatively small markets.

Despite these additional potential moat sources, wide economic moats are still hard to come by for commodity processors. Those that stand the best chance at building durable moats are the companies with hard-to-copy processes or technologies, patents backed by robust R&D pipelines, and deep customer relationships that create high switching costs.

Chemical conglomerate BASF is an example of a commodity processor that has built a narrow moat from two sources: cost advantage and intangible assets. For starters, we think BASF holds a slight cost advantage in the production of chemicals. This advantage is not built on access to cheap raw materials, but rather stems from the company's scale and its unique Verbund production process. BASF uses the "Verbund" moniker to label its massive chemical production complexes around the world. The company operates six Verbund sites: two each in Europe, North America, and Asia.

To give an idea of the scale of these operations, the firm's German Verbund site includes 160 chemical production plants and employs more than 35,000 people, with a total site area of 10 square kilometers. By grouping many different chemical plants close together and vertically integrating production, BASF saves on transportation costs, consumes less energy, and enjoys higher product yields. For example, by-products from one plant can be used as raw materials at another. This concept extends to energy use as well, where heat from production processes at one plant can be captured and used for energy at an adjacent plant. The company estimates that the Verbund concept cuts costs annually by roughly EUR 1 billion—a meaningful amount considering 2012 operating income was roughly EUR 6.7 billion. Although many other chemical companies operate world-class facilities that generate economies of scale at the individual plant level, very few, if any, match BASF's Verbund concept of linking numerous plants together at one site.

In addition to cost advantage, a portion of BASF's narrow economic moat is built from intangible assets. Over the past decade or so, the company has shifted its product mix more toward specialty chemicals. Specialty chemicals generate more pricing power with customers than basic chemical products do, creating higher margins. BASF also consistently pours money into research and development, creating patented products that typically generate pricing power.

Despite these advantages, we hesitate to award BASF a wide economic moat because we think the company's Verbund scale advantage could be sufficiently replicated over a longer period of time. If enough chemical mega-complexes were ultimately built around the globe, BASF's cost advantage would diminish. We believe this possibility is far enough in the future, though, that we do feel BASF has earned a narrow economic moat.

Key considerations to remember when analyzing commodity processors:

- Does the company have sustainable access to low cost inputs? A company may have a temporary advantage with access to lower cost inputs based on regional pricing, but that advantage may not be sustainable over the long run.
- Does the company produce an ultraspecialized product or control a proprietary production process? Look for the ability of others to replicate a product or process over time. If decades have passed without competitors figuring out the magic bullet, then the company likely has a moat. A proprietary production process can lead to a cost advantage.
- Do the company's research and development efforts support a portfolio of patented products? Assess the product portfolio and the firm's R&D pipeline.
- Do the company's specialized products or distribution model create switching costs? Look for consistent pricing power related to switching costs as well as the amount of interaction between the commodity processor and the customer, or a potential geographic advantage.
- What is the mix of moatworthy businesses within a company? Often large commodity processors will have several disparate segments with some holding sustainable competitive advantages and others not.

Metals and Mining

In the metals and mining industry, competitive advantage generally comes down to geology. World-class deposits are unique assets, and favorable geology typically translates to a favorable position relative to other producers in the industry.

When assessing geology, three rules of thumb usually hold true: Bigger is better, higher grades mean higher profits, and complex processing requirements increase costs. First, size—in the form of large seams or massive pits—drives economies of scale. Some miners scrape away at deposits that are hundreds of feet thick, while others must precisely chip away at veins less than a foot thick. All else equal, the former is preferred. Next, high-grade deposits mean less rock needs to get moved for each unit of the desired metal (grade measures the concentration of metal per unit of rock). Finally, processing requirements determine how much of the metal can actually be separated from the rock (this is the practice of metallurgy). It's all part of an equation that determines how much effort is needed to produce each unit of output, and the denominator in the equation of total costs over output is a powerful force. Simply put, look for scalable resources, high grades, and simple metallurgy. As a final point, be mindful of acquisition costs. Whether a miner acquires a land package from a government or through the acquisition of another publicly traded company, paying too high a price can destroy the economics, no matter how attractive the geology.

Mining company Potash Corporation of Saskatchewan is one of the few basic materials companies that we believe has a wide economic moat, thanks to both low-cost potash assets and high barriers to entry created by staggering greenfield capital costs. PotashCorp is on the low end of the potash cost curve, allowing the company to pump out profits even if potash prices should approach marginal costs of production in the future. Lower costs stem from the geology of the company's Canadian deposits and partially from the scale of its mines.

In addition to lower-than-average cash costs, PotashCorp also benefits from barriers to entry in the potash market. Economically viable deposits are found in only a handful of locations around the globe, with Canada, Russia, and Belarus as the main producing regions. PotashCorp's brownfield expansions come at much lower capital costs per ton than proposed greenfield projects. Greenfield projects can take more than seven years to complete and fully ramp up, creating a significant barrier to entry for new participants.

Finally, we believe PotashCorp will be able to produce potash for many years to come, with reserve lives for its mines ranging from 65 to 85 years at current production levels. This long production life combined with a solid operating and capital-cost profile makes us comfortable awarding PotashCorp a wide moat rating.

Key considerations for metals and mining companies:

- Does the company own or control geological deposits or other natural resources with advantageous characteristics? Consider specifics such as grade, stripping ratios or overburden, mining method, processing needs, and recovery rates. How rare or prevalent are deposits or other natural resources of high quality?

- Does the company benefit from economies of scale? Which costs are fixed and therefore leverageable? Companies with individual assets that have higher production capacities than those of other players in the industry can benefit from spreading fixed costs over higher volume, which results in lower per-unit costs. Having large total capacity in a small geographic region may also result in economies of scale if the individual producing assets are closely integrated and can share costs and resources as with a single plant or mine.
- Does the company benefit from low transportation costs? What is the cost of transportation relative to total costs or the price of the product? Because of the materiality of transportation costs, producers located closest to customers can have a significant cost advantage relative to far-flung competitors.
- Is this company subject to favorable or unfavorable political regimes? Does the company pay higher royalties or taxes than other players in the industry? What is the risk of future partial or full expropriation? Conversely, does the government help the company maintain a sustainable cost advantage, for example, through barriers to entry? It's not a given that the economic rents generated by advantaged natural resources will flow to shareholders of publicly traded companies rather than governments. Companies will often spend capital to develop a natural resource only to find that the rules of the game have changed once production starts, usually through higher taxes or royalties than those agreed on during the development phases. This results in higher costs for the producer, which can offset any natural-resource-based or transportation-cost advantages. Other times, the valuable asset will be outright expropriated by the government. When that risk is high, we're hesitant to award a narrow or wide economic moat rating.

10

Consumer

If you want to know whether brand matters to consumers, just ask a few people if they drink Coke or Pepsi, smoke Marlboros or Camels, eat Heinz ketchup or Hunt's, or buy certain brands of beauty and hygiene products or just go with whatever generic product they happen to see. Brand matters tremendously to many consumers, and when consumers are willing to pay a premium to get the brand they want, brands serve as a powerful source of competitive advantage. As a result, brands serve as the predominant source of economic moats for many consumer-focused companies.

Beyond the intangible asset of brand power, a few other moat sources also come into play for the diverse consumer sector, as Figure 10.1 illustrates. Cost advantage is a fairly common one. Take the large beverage companies, for example. Because they're buying such huge quantities of sweeteners, juices, and packaging materials, they benefit from economies of scale and bargaining power that lower their costs relative to smaller peers. The network effect can also help some consumer companies, such as online retailers, where low

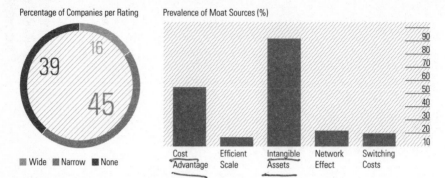

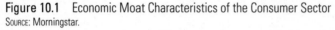

Figure 10.1   Economic Moat Characteristics of the Consumer Sector
SOURCE: Morningstar.

prices and an expansive breadth of products attract millions of customers, which in turn attract third-party merchants to the online retailers' marketplaces. Additionally, customer reviews and product recommendations increase in relevance as more customers and products are added to the platform, strengthening the network effect.

Beverages

In the beverage industry—which includes makers of soft drinks, beer, wine, and spirits—generating consistent excess returns requires strong brands supported by vast distribution networks. Large beverage companies benefit from a virtuous cycle: The largest brands can also most efficiently invest in marketing programs, bottling facilities, and supply-chain operations, spurring further growth and profits. This virtuous cycle has allowed soft-drink giant Coca-Cola, beer juggernaut Anheuser-Busch, and spirits leader Diageo to sell premium-priced drinks through the most efficiently run distribution networks, capturing leading market shares in the process. These large firms also enjoy buying power, purchasing needed supplies at better rates than their smaller peers can.

Brand loyalty is also strong for many beverage categories. This loyalty reduces searching costs for consumers and enables beverage companies to launch product-line extensions (such as Diet Pepsi, Coke Zero, or Budweiser Platinum), as well as different packaging sizes to meet the needs of different channels and different drinking occasions. The strongest beverage brands enjoy premium pricing, helping ensure meaningful return on invested capital, or ROIC.

Thanks to these competitive advantages, many of the big beverage companies boast wide economic moats, and likely will for decades to come. It would be extremely expensive and time-consuming for second-tier beverage companies or new competitors to leap-frog today's leading firms. It takes decades to build out brands and distribution systems, and consumer preferences change slowly. What's more, several narrow-moat beverage companies, such as Dr Pepper Snapple Group and Monster Beverage, depend on wide-moat firms for distribution. This dependence allows the wide-moat firms to reap additional income from their smaller rivals.

Key considerations for evaluating beverage companies:

- Do the firm's brands command a price premium relative to competitors?
- How easily could the distribution system be replicated?
- Is the brand likely to lose, maintain, or increase market share over the coming years? Eroding share could signal heightened competition and diminished pricing power.
- Healthy margins and return on invested capital may indicate that the firm possesses a cost advantage in the form of a more efficient distribution network, bottling facilities, and supply chain operations.

Consumer Products

Within the diverse consumer products industry—which includes companies that manufacture, market, and distribute a variety of food, household, and personal care products—strong brand portfolios and low-cost operating platforms are the main sources of economic moats. It takes ample time and resources to achieve the economies of scale that dominant consumer product firms possess, creating high barriers to entry for new participants. This scale ultimately leads to lower production and distribution costs per unit relative to smaller peers.

Wide-moat firms in this industry must exhibit dominant brand portfolios, expansive global scale, and the ability to compete in categories where private-label offerings have failed to gain significant penetration. Companies with narrow moats are generally lacking in at least one of these areas. Leading consumer product firms invest heavily in product innovation and marketing support for core brands to ensure that their products resonate with consumers, enhancing their competitive positioning relative to peers. Firms that compete in commoditylike categories (where products are fast-turning and often perishable, like meat and dairy) generally don't have economic moats, as these firms are price takers with minimal differentiation.

Campbell Soup Company, the largest producer of soup in the world, is an example of a wide-moat consumer products firm. Campbell's moat rests in the unrivaled economies of scale that result from its leading and highly profitable U.S. soup business, as well as its strong brand and expansive global distribution network. Campbell controls just under 60% of the domestic wet soup market, and we've been impressed by how profitable this dominant position has proven to be. Operating margins in this category (which represents about one third of Campbell's total sales and more than half of operating profits) are north of 20%—much higher than other categories in the packaged food industry. In addition, Campbell has generated returns on invested capital (including goodwill) of around 18% on average over the past 10 years, more than double our 8.1% cost-of-capital estimate, supporting our take that the firm maintains a wide economic moat.

Key considerations for evaluating consumer product companies:

- What is the brand strength within the company's portfolio? Volume and pricing metrics over time are usually indicators of brand strength. Having a number-one or number-two market-share position in a specific category generally requires a strong brand.
- Does the company possess significant scale, which subsequently enables it to maintain a lower cost of production and distribution than its peers? Scale can be on a local or international basis, but it's important to determine whether its network is so vast that it would be costly and time-consuming for a new entrant to replicate.
- To what degree have private-label offerings penetrated the category? Even if private-label products maintain ample share, that doesn't necessarily imply that brand strength is fleeting. However, continuous branded product innovation is that much more essential and must be viewed by the consumer as value-added.
- We tend to include goodwill when looking at returns on invested capital, because consumer product companies have been highly acquisitive in the past, and we don't expect that to change in the future. Firms are exhibiting a penchant to build out their global footprint and offset slower growth in

more-mature developed markets. Acquisitions should not prevent companies from earning ROICs in excess of weighted average cost of capital, or WACC, after goodwill has been taken into consideration.

Tobacco

For better or worse, tobacco companies enjoy big profits and wide economic moats that don't seem in danger of eroding any time soon (what's good for investors isn't always good for consumers).

Strong brands and addictive products are key components of tobacco firms' well-entrenched moats. Smokers tend to be quite loyal to their brands of choice, and given the addictive nature of nicotine, tobacco users typically keep buying their favorite brands even in the face of steady price increases or lower-cost alternatives. Premium brand Marlboro, for example (owned by Altria in the United States and Philip Morris International in the rest of the world) holds the leading market share in many countries despite the prevalence of lower-priced cigarettes. Thanks to this robust pricing power combined with effective cost-control efforts, tobacco firms have been able to increase operating margins in recent years, despite continued volume declines in the United States.

Tobacco firms also typically benefit from scale. In most countries, only a handful of tobacco companies dominate the vast majority of the market. Consequently, they can collectively flex their power when negotiating with their suppliers (tobacco leaf growers, filter suppliers, paper and packaging vendors) or obtaining retail shelf space. In many markets, the incumbent cigarette manufacturers also benefit from governmental barriers to entry. In the United States, for example, the U.S. Food and Drug Administration, or FDA, has been extremely slow to approve any new tobacco products—a regulatory hurdle that keeps new competitors at bay.

Key considerations for evaluating tobacco companies:

- Will pricing be sufficient to offset the impact of falling cigarette volumes? Despite falling U.S. volumes, cigarettes have had tremendous pricing power and the profit pool has steadily grown. However, this may not always be the case.
- Are the competitors behaving rationally? Aggressive pricing activity to spur volume growth could have negative consequences on returns on invested

capital industrywide. Will tobacco alternatives, such as e-cigarettes, be disruptive to the cigarette sector? Although we believe cigarette alternatives will garner only modest share, should e-cigs capture meaningful share (20%-plus) of the cigarette market, it is possible that big tobacco's market shares within e-cigs will not be comparable to their shares of the traditional cigarette market.

- Will changes in governmental regulation and taxation drastically alter the industry or result in increased price competition? Governments could cause shocks to the tobacco sector either by drastic increases in excise taxes, or implementation of new regulations (such as plain packaging or banning menthol). Depending on the governmental actions taken, tobacco companies may see a deterioration of their competitive positioning and an increased prevalence of bootleg or counterfeit products.

Restaurants

The massive restaurant industry, which generates nearly $2 trillion in annual revenue, can be split into quick-service restaurants, where patrons pay at a counter and receive their meals, and casual-dining restaurants, where seated customers place orders with servers.

Nonexistent switching costs, fierce industry competition, and low barriers to entry make it difficult for restaurant operators to establish economic moats. However, we believe a handful of restaurant operators have carved out moats through a mix of intangible assets and cost advantages. The restaurant category is home to some of the most widely recognized brands across the globe, thanks to their vast networks of convenient restaurant locations, a consistent customer experience, and largely uniform menus with some geographic variations. Larger restaurant chains also possess economies of scale and wield considerable influence over suppliers, ensuring access to food and other raw materials at predictable, competitive prices. These cost advantages allow restaurant operators to maintain pricing parity with smaller rivals—even those that resort to aggressive promotional tactics—and still produce greater profit margins.

The limited number of restaurant operators with wide moats (currently just McDonald's and Starbucks) have intangible assets in brands that are recognized almost everywhere across the globe (often allowing the restaurant company to charge premium prices for a commodity product), cohesive franchise systems, a track record of menu innovation across multiple dayparts, or segments of the day, and commitment to remodeling restaurant locations on a regular basis (every five to seven years). Wide-moat players also typically have category-leading margins, supported by meaningful cost advantages such as bargaining clout with suppliers and advertising economies of scale. Narrow-moat operators typically possess a mix of strong brand recognition and cost advantages, though these qualities are often restricted to one or two key markets and do not necessarily apply on a global basis.

Dunkin' Brands, home to the familiar Dunkin' Donuts and Baskin-Robbins brands, is one of the quick-service restaurant companies that lands in narrow-moat territory. Dunkin's moat owes mainly to its well-known brand and a cohesive franchisee system, particularly in its core Northeastern U.S. markets (where approximately 70% of the Dunkin' Donuts U.S. locations are located). In recent years, Dunkin' has been able to increase menu prices and shift sales toward premium-priced and limited-time offerings. In addition, Dunkin's U.S. franchisees remain healthy, evidenced by relatively low franchisee bankruptcy rates and cash-on-cash returns among the highest in the quick-service restaurant industry.

Given Dunkin's considerable presence in the Northeastern U.S. and emerging awareness across the U.S. and other international markets, we believe the company has some influence over suppliers, which helps provide access to food and other raw materials at competitive prices. However, as measured by systemwide sales, Dunkin' remains the distant number-two player in the U.S. beverage-snack restaurant category market (behind Starbucks) and the number-seven player in the U.S. quick-service restaurant market, making it difficult to argue that Dunkin' has a more favorable bargaining position with suppliers than its peers do. Additionally, while franchisee restaurant build-out costs have contracted over the past several years, we do not think they differ materially from the rest of the quick-service restaurant industry. Thus, we don't consider cost advantages to be a source of Dunkin's moat.

Key considerations for evaluating restaurant companies:

- Does the brand possess enough pricing power to offset food and labor cost inflation? If the restaurant operator can maintain restaurant transaction counts and operating margins after raising prices, the brand may possess sufficient pricing power to support an economic moat.

- How has the company historically fared during price wars? Because switching costs are nonexistent, the restaurant industry has a long history of price wars. If a restaurant operator has been able to preserve operating margins during periods of aggressive industry discounting, the firm's cost advantages may indicate an economic moat.
- Has the restaurant concept been successfully replicated across multiple markets? If the restaurant operator continues to increase unit counts across multiple markets while also improving underlying margins, this may suggest intangible-asset or scale-related cost advantages worthy of a moat.
- Is the restaurant franchise system cohesive? For a restaurant franchisor that collects royalties on franchisee sales, the intangible-asset moat source depends on the overall health of its franchisees. Signals of a strong franchise system include a company's willingness to provide franchisees with capital for remodeling projects and new equipment, low franchisee bankruptcy rates, and robust franchisor cash flow.

Retail Defensive

Defensive retailers are companies involved with purchasing, warehousing, transporting, stocking, marketing, and selling a variety of branded and unbranded consumer products (usually nonexclusive consumer staples), mainly through retail store networks. Some firms manufacture their own products and several offer additional products and services, ranging from gasoline and pharmaceuticals to banking services.

Cost advantages and intangible assets (brands) are the key drivers of moats in the retail defensive industry. In grocery stores, discount stores, and pharmaceutical retailers, these moat sources typically play off one another: A brand-driven moat can emerge from a cost advantage (think Wal-Mart and its strong reputation as the low-cost leader), while a truly differentiated store concept may allow a firm to charge higher prices and achieve enough scale to create a cost advantage (think Whole Foods and its wide array of premium-priced products). Cost advantages that fuel a brand moat often result from purchasing scale that allows a retailer to obtain more favorable pricing from suppliers. Retailers can then pass these cost savings on to the consumer, sometimes accepting little to no profit on traffic drivers (loss leaders like milk and bread) with other higher-margin products or membership fees more than compensating—a model well used by Costco Wholesale. Alternatively, low-cost retailers can maintain similar prices while enjoying higher margins than higher-cost peers.

Most defensive retailers do not have economic moats, but larger firms can receive narrow or wide ratings if they have clear and sustainable cost leadership. In these situations, the combination of (virtually) unrivaled scale and brand loyalty reduces the threat posed by potential new entrants and aggressive pricing actions by competitors. Narrow-moat firms typically have enough scale and name recognition to compete with the industry leaders, but lack the scale economies or cost advantages possessed by larger players with lower per-unit costs.

Wal-Mart is the classic example of a mega-retailer with a wide moat stemming from the high-volume purchasing power generated by its massive scale. As the largest retailer in the world, Wal-Mart has tremendous leverage to extract the most favorable terms possible from consumer-goods suppliers, vendors, and manufacturers. Moreover, to gain access to the largest sales channel in retail, suppliers must tie into Wal-Mart's just-in-time inventory and logistics systems.

Key considerations for evaluating retail defensive companies:

- Does the company have a relative cost advantage? A firm with greater market share or retail distribution processes that eliminate unnecessary components of the industry supply chain can lower per-unit costs enough to create a cost advantage.
- What is the firm's product mix, and how much purchasing scale does it have over category suppliers? If a retailer is the source of a high percentage of revenue or profit for a particular supplier and there are adequate substitutes, the retailer may have negotiating leverage. However, a retailer may have relative purchasing scale in some categories but not others, depending on the scope and scale of purchasing in each.
- What is the risk of a new entrant, alternative channel, or innovative format stealing considerable market share? Firms with an established multichannel presence are more insulated from competitive threats posed by new and more-efficient channels. Retailers without an online presence, category dominance, or a low-cost warehouse format are often disadvantaged.
- How does the company's store base and customer demographic compare or overlap with those of competitors? Firms that have large target customer demographic overlap with large competitors could face fierce price competition.

Specialty Retail

Specialty retail—which includes a broad range of retail categories including auto parts, books, consumer electronics, home furnishings, home improvement supplies, office supplies, online retailers, pet supplies, and sporting goods— is one of the most challenging consumer industries for developing moats. Specialty retailers generally lack the clout with suppliers or scale advantages to compete with large retailers like Wal-Mart, Costco, or Amazon on a price leadership basis, forcing players to explore other ways to differentiate their products or shopping experiences. Because there are virtually no switching costs in the specialty retail category, the only way a merchant can establish a moat is by offering something that keeps consumers shopping at its stores or websites rather than those of competitors. Many specialty retailers tout technical expertise or installation services as a source of differentiation, though we've found that these rarely provide consumers enough incentive to pay higher prices. There are a few exceptions (pet grooming and boarding services or do-it-yourself automotive parts in the U.S., for instance), but the majority of specialty retailers do not have any sustainable competitive advantages.

For the handful of specialty retailers with moats, the competitive advantage usually stems from intangible assets (specialized or premium product assortments, or unique service offerings) or cost advantages (logistics efficiencies or significant bargaining power with vendors regarding product procurement, advertising, and rent). We believe unique service offerings allow some specialty retailers to price products at a modest premium to mass merchants, while specialty retailers with cost advantages can instill customer loyalty by passing along a portion of savings to consumers in the form of lower everyday pricing.

PetSmart is one of the few specialty retailers that has earned a narrow economic moat. As the largest specialty pet retailer, PetSmart benefits from significant scale advantages over its most direct rivals. Management has commented that PetSmart's prices are generally 8%–10% lower than both specialty retail and grocery store competitors. Additionally, the company offers a wide array of services that are not economical for smaller competitors to replicate. PetSmart's products are pricier than those at discount retailers, but we believe this premium pricing is sustainable. Although a segment of the population will always gravitate to the low-cost provider, PetSmart has successfully differentiated itself to its relatively affluent target audience. These consumers earn more, spend more on pet-related goods, and are less price-sensitive when shopping for pet products. As a result, PetSmart is able to consistently charge a modest surcharge by creating a pleasant, differentiated shopping experience. The firm's specialized outlets offer an unrivaled selection of premium consumable products, unique services, and specialized customer service. PetSmart has also locked in agreements with several of its premium vendors, restricting the vendor from distributing certain products to discount and grocery retailers. All of these elements enhance the PetSmart brand and help the firm attract the most profitable pet owner. Additionally, PetSmart has successfully leveraged its brand and scale to push its own premium private-label brands, which are higher-margin items.

Key considerations for evaluating specialty retailers:

- Is the retailer's product assortment or shopping experience differentiated? Most specialty retailers offer homogenous, commoditized product assortments, and consumers tend to gravitate to price leaders when making purchase decisions (often mass merchants or large online retailers) unless the product assortment, shopping experience, or customer service offerings are truly differentiated.
- How concentrated is the retail category? For those retailers that have a specialized product assortment that is difficult for mass merchants to replicate, market share data and industry consolidation trends can signal intangible-asset and cost-advantage moat sources. Larger players in more concentrated retail categories (home improvement, auto parts) tend to have meaningful scale advantages relative to retailers in fragmented categories (sporting goods).
- If the company is an online retailer, does it possess a network effect? Online retailers sometimes exhibit a network effect, where the value of the network to the online retailer and its third-party fulfillment partners grows as the number of people who use the network increases. Though each geography brings its own set of characteristics and regulations, we tend to see a network effect when approximately 15% or more of the local population are active users of the online retailer.[1]

Lodging

In the lodging industry, there are three types of companies, each with a different revenue model: (1) Hotel franchisors generate fees from franchisees in their system; (2) hotel managers generate fees from management services provided to hotel owners; and (3) owned-hotel operators generate revenue directly from business and leisure travelers.

The lodging industry is one of the few areas in the consumer space where switching costs come into play. Companies that manage and franchise hotels have sticky long-term management and franchise agreements, typically 10 to 30 years in duration, which have high switching costs for hotel owners. If a hotel owner exits a company's system before a contract expires, the hotel owner faces a disruption to business operations, as well as significant contract termination fees and expenditures to renovate and rebrand a property to meet new brand specifications. The long duration of contracts and low attrition among hotel owners in managed and franchised hotel systems have historically enabled such operators to generate excess returns. Managed and franchised hotel operators can also benefit from a network effect, where the value of the network to the hotel operator grows as the number of franchisees in the network increases.

Although these moat sources have created narrow moats for a number of hotel companies, intense competition has prevented us from assigning wide moat ratings in this industry. The key factors we consider when deciding whether a lodging company's moat is narrow or wide include the following: (1) the average length of the company's contracts; (2) the engagement level of consumers with the firm's rewards networks; and (3) the mix of premium versus budget rooms within its system. First, hotel contracts range from 10 to 30 years, with the majority less than 20 years, meaning it's difficult to have confidence that returns will persist long enough for wide-moat status. Second, some hotels have sizable rewards networks with millions of nominal members, but very small populations of active participants, highlighting a low level of consumer engagement and intense industry competition. Third, some of the most active franchisers have large room systems of budget hotel brands where competition is fiercest and price tends to be a more important factor than brand.

Key considerations for evaluating lodging companies:

- Does the company primarily manage or franchise hotels, or primarily own its hotels? In assessing whether a hotel company has an economic moat, determine the percentage of the number of rooms in the company's portfolio and the percentage of revenue that are derived from managed and franchised hotels (which bring high franchisee switching costs, and network effect) versus company-owned locations.

- Is a company concentrated in a specific geography, or does the company have a global operation with hotels in multiple continents? A company with a global brand generally benefits more from a network effect and brand loyalty than a small regional operator does.
- Is the company pursuing an "asset-light" strategy of divesting owned hotels and converting them to management and franchise contracts, or is it pursuing acquisitions of owned hotels?
- What percentages of the company's pipeline are owned, managed, and franchised?
- What is the company's revenue per available room, or revPAR index for the market segment it focuses on? Does the company generate higher revPAR than average for the markets it is focused on?

Notes

1. Percentage based on a Morningstar study of active user bases for online retailers across multiple geographies from 1995 through 2012.

11

Energy

Even in this age of increased interest in alternative and renewable energy sources, the global energy industry remains heavily focused on fossil fuels and is dominated by companies aiming to seek, find, extract, process, and distribute oil and natural gas.

Not surprisingly, commodity prices have a major influence on the energy industry. The sector is highly cyclical, with small changes in supply and demand having big effects on commodity prices and short-term company profits. However, the cyclical peaks and valleys don't tend to last very long—something to keep in mind when investing in this sector.

It's not always easy for energy companies to create long-term moats in a sector that's so strongly affected by commodity prices, but it is possible. In fact, there are quite a few energy companies with moats, but the moat landscape varies dramatically depending on the type of energy firm in question. Moats are especially rare among drillers, for example, where price trumps most other considerations for customers. A decent number of exploration and production,

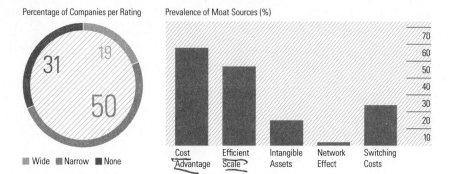

Percentage of Companies per Rating   Prevalence of Moat Sources (%)

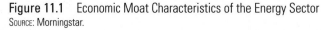

Wide   Narrow   None

Cost Advantage   Efficient Scale   Intangible Assets   Network Effect   Switching Costs

Figure 11.1   Economic Moat Characteristics of the Energy Sector
SOURCE: Morningstar.

or E&P, companies and refiners have been able to establish narrow moats, primarily through cost advantage, which is the most common moat source for the energy sector, as Figure 11.1 shows. E&Ps build a cost advantage by developing oil and gas properties with long-lived reserves, multiple years of drilling inventory, and favorable well economics. Refiners can gain cost advantage over global peers through access to low-cost crude oil, lower operating costs, and the ability to export refined products.

Wide moats in the energy sector occur most often among midstream oil and gas pipeline companies, which usually build their moats through efficient scale. Both regulation and economics tend to limit competition for existing pipelines, and while competition for new pipeline projects can be fierce, it also tends to be rational, with long-term contracts designed to project a modest, but steady, return on capital for years.

Oil and Gas Drilling

Oil and gas drillers, which provide rigs, crews, and the associated drilling services to oil and gas firms on a day-rate contract basis, generally do not have moats. Drillers operate in a very tough environment where price drives decision making among customers, although intangibles such as quality of service, operational and technical expertise, equipment suitability and availability, reputation, and the driller's safety record are also considered. Demand for drilling rigs depends on customer expectations around commodity prices in the near future and the expected economics of their projects, while supply is a function of new-build prices, ability to access the capital markets, crew availability, and the individual driller's fleet needs. Given the different demand and supply drivers, there are frequent mismatches between supply and demand, resulting in a highly cyclical industry, where day rates (the total cost of a drilling contract divided by the number of days in the contract) can swing more than 50% during a cycle.

Despite the difficult industry dynamics, the largest offshore drillers do enjoy substantial competitive advantages over their smaller peers, but very limited or no advantages over their closest major peers because of similar fleet sizes and composition. These advantages don't generally apply to onshore drillers, a more fragmented industry with lower barriers to entry (cheaper rigs, more crew availability). Larger rig fleets provide major offshore drillers with several intangible assets, including financial stability throughout the decades-long project cycle, the ability to match an experienced crew with a new rig, and more rig options to meet a customer's requirements, as well as a strong reputation and an excellent safety record. Replicating this type of expertise is difficult, as it can take several years and up to $750 million to construct an ultra-deep-water rig, and experienced engineers are in short supply.

An always-aging asset base and an intensely competitive market mean that wide moats are extremely unlikely for drillers. An experienced crew's full value can be tapped only with a suitably advanced rig, and deep-water technology is rapidly advancing. So, while a rig's useful life may be 30 years, its useful life as a leading-edge rig is much shorter—a situation that creates uncertainty in terms of duration of any excess returns. Moreover, the highly consolidated market structure promotes an intense competitive rivalry between the largest drillers, making it difficult for us to have the degree of confidence required to award moats.

Transocean Ltd. is one driller that has beaten the odds and achieved a narrow moat, thanks to its specialization in ultra-deep-water drilling, where rigs typically drill in depths of 10,000 feet or more. Operating costs can top $1 million a day, and the ability to limit unplanned drilling downtime is immensely valuable for customers. Transocean owns twice the number of deep-water rigs as its closest peer and is by far the most experienced deep-water driller. Its specialization in this challenging drilling market lets it charge a day-rate premium. Also, because of the time and money required to build a new rig, it would be difficult for peers to close the size and experience gap with Transocean. If competitors were to merge to try to challenge Transocean's deep-water dominance, Transocean could still retain some advantages, as it has typically dictated the industry's best drilling practices and has patented many of its efforts.

A few other considerations to keep in mind when evaluating drillers:

- How large is the premium asset base—deep-water rigs, in this instance? A large number of specialized deep-water rigs provides a stable stream of income and also indicates a hard-to-duplicate collection of drilling expertise.
- What is the size and makeup of the driller's rig construction program (if it exists)? A careful review of factors such as rig cost, the yards being used, delivery dates, contract status, and the existence of any additional rig options is useful for evaluating a driller.
- What is the balance sheet like, and how is the driller using it? A driller's leverage levels and pursuit of unusual financing options such as master limited partnerships can provide insight into future rig ordering trends and thus affect an assessment of the driller's ability to build a premium asset base and potentially capture economic profits.

Oil and Gas Exploration and Production

Exploration and production companies are firms that possess the rights to harvest commodities from geological deposits. These companies explore for deposits, develop oil and gas fields, and produce commodities for sale.

Cost advantage is the main potential moat source for E&P companies. Because these companies are producing undifferentiated commodities that are in many cases widely fungible, the ability to produce at a cost well below the prevailing price is the only real option for generating economic profits. Geological characteristics are the most important determinants of extraction costs. In extremely oversimplified terms, E&Ps benefit from encountering more resources per rock, closer to the surface, and in thicker and larger formations.

Wide moat ratings are rare among E&P firms. These companies depend on geological deposits—finite resources that eventually deplete. To even maintain production levels, let alone grow, E&Ps must eventually find or acquire and then develop additional reserves. The only potential candidates for wide-moat ratings would be low-cost producers with long reserve lives, where production levels can be maintained based on current reserve or resource bases for decades to come. For narrow moats, we must expect positive excess returns for at least a decade with no substantial threat of major value destruction. This precludes a wide moat for any E&P company that operates in a politically risky jurisdiction where future profits may flow to the powers that be, no matter how attractive the company's deposits are.

Range Resources is an example of an E&P company that has earned a narrow moat. Based in Fort Worth, Texas, Range has an edge over its peers in three dimensions of asset quality that are important in the E&P space: resource potential (the number of available drilling locations and the amount of recoverable hydrocarbons at each location), per-unit production cost (which takes into account royalties, leasehold outlays, drilling and completion costs, lifting expenses, and taxes), and realized prices (which are affected by the mix of oil versus gas as well as regional differentials). Range controls more than two decades of drilling inventory across the Pennsylvania Marcellus shale, where the company is targeting both dry gas and liquids-rich formations. This acreage features low operating and development costs, favorable price differentials given proximity to northeastern U.S. customers, the potential to develop multiple productive horizons, and, based on planned infrastructure build-out over the next few years, sufficient capacity to bring production to market. As an early mover and sizable operator in this region, Range also benefits from low royalty rates, blocked-up acreage positions, and established relationships with service providers and midstream partners.

A few other considerations to keep in mind when evaluating E&P companies:

- When looking for cost advantage among E&P companies, try to understand not only a company's current cost profile, but also its future costs. In forecasting future costs, it's important to incorporate all relevant outlays, including lease and permit costs, all payments to service and equipment providers, development expenditures, production expenses, and royalties. It's also best to use a price forecast that reflects a "normal" environment, absent supply-and-demand shocks that lead to unsustainably high or low commodity prices. When it comes to prices, the realized price a company garners for its production is what matters, not some global benchmark. Realizations can vary depending on product quality, processing needs, transportation distances, and infrastructure capabilities.

- Does the company have low capital costs? Consider finding and development costs per unit; depreciation, depletion, and amortization costs per unit can be used as a proxy. In oil and gas, pay special attention to whether undeveloped reserves have been included in the denominator, as undeveloped reserves are less valuable and will cost more to develop than proven developed reserves.
- Does the company have low production costs? These may also be called *cash costs*.
- What is the company's reserve life in years? This may also be called an *R/P ratio* because it's calculated by taking total reserves and dividing by annual production. It's one indication of sustainability.
- When looking at returns on invested capital, we usually include goodwill in the denominator. Resource acquisition costs must be considered when determining a company's ability to generate economic profits for shareholders.

Oil and Gas Midstream

Midstream oil and gas companies are those involved with processing, transporting, and storing natural gas, natural gas liquids, crude oil, and refined products. There are multiple ways for these midstream companies to build moats, but efficient scale is the dominant source. Although the competition is fierce among midstream firms for new projects, once a pipeline is in service, it typically enjoys excess returns. A long-haul pipeline is an inherently moaty asset, thanks to regulatory oversight and market dynamics, which tend to deter the construction of competing pipelines unless a clear economic case can be made for a new line. Even then, the incumbent pipeline has an advantage because it's typically more affordable for a firm to add capacity through pumps or compression or add a parallel line using the same rights-of-way as the existing pipe than it is for a competitor to secure rights-of-way and construct a new line. Midstream firms typically seek to lock in project economics through long-term contracts with shippers before ever breaking ground on a new project, ensuring that, at a minimum, project and capital costs are recouped, with potential for excess returns over time.

Although a single pipeline can be attractive, a network of pipelines— serving multiple end markets and supplied by multiple producing regions—is much more valuable. Price differentials, or gaps created by location or time, can be an important factor in midstream companies' earnings potential. These firms can optimize the flow of oil or gas across their systems to meet producer or end-user demand while locking in geographic price differentials, or they can use storage facilities tied to the network to lock in price differentials across time periods. Midstream assets also benefit from high customer switching costs, as oil and gas production upstream of these assets typically has few or no alternatives to using these assets.

The majority of the midstream pipeline companies we cover actually have wide economic moats. Smaller firms tend to be less competitive than larger firms with tightly integrated assets because the larger companies can compete more effectively on price and service. Firms that can provide services across multiple links of the midstream value chain are particularly well positioned. For example, a company that operates a gathering system, a processing plant, a natural gas pipeline system serving multiple markets, and a natural gas liquids pipeline system connecting the processing plant to downstream markets—such as Enterprise Products—has a much greater opportunity to earn fees than a simple gatherer-processor of natural gas, such as Regency Energy. Integration along the value chain can also ensure higher capacity utilization across a pipeline network. For this reason we tend to award wide economic moats to the larger, vertically integrated midstream firms.

Key considerations to keep in mind for midstream oil and gas firms:

- Does a midstream firm currently realize excess returns? Does the firm possess an interlinked network of assets, either geographically or across the value chain?
- How well do the assets of a midstream firm complement each other? Does the firm integrate across the midstream value chain; is it able to collect rents at each link in which it operates?
- Where is incremental capital spending being directed? Can the firm deploy capital on projects that increase throughput across multiple assets? Does a firm's investment bolster its competitive position in a given region or basin, or provide strategic entry into a new market or geography?

Refining

Refiners are in the business of converting crude oil ("feedstock" in industry parlance) into usable products such as gasoline, diesel, and jet fuel. It's a highly competitive industry with no differentiation among products and little control over input or output costs, so access to discounted crude, often referred to as cost-advantaged feedstock, becomes the most valuable competitive edge a refiner can have. Generally, this advantage can come in two forms. One is proximity to crude production or access to stranded crude that allows the refiner to enjoy a discount relative to the international benchmark and thereby increase margins. The other is a refiner's ability to process low-quality, heavy, sour crude, with high complexity, that trades at a discount to light, sweet crude that's easier to process. The first source is harder to come by because the conditions that determine the discount are largely out of the refiner's control. The second is easier to obtain but generally requires significant investment on the part of the refiner. As a result, the first type of advantage is preferable and holds the potential for higher returns given the relative lack of investment in upgrading capacity needed to realize the advantage.

Refiners can hold several other competitive advantages, which would be insufficient to create a moat on their own, but can strengthen an existing moat. First, a refiner can realize lower operating costs than those of its peers. This results most often from lower energy costs, usually concerning domestic natural gas, which can make up almost half of cash operating costs. Second, refiners with the ability to export can improve margins by commanding higher prices than those available in the domestic market or by running at higher utilization rates, lowering fixed costs per barrel. Finally, a refiner can hold marketing and distribution assets, such as retail gas stations, which can ensure an outlet for production and result in higher utilization rates for refiners in markets with declining demand or excess supply.

Questions around sustainability of crude oil discounts generally prevent refiners from earning wide moats. Given the ever-changing nature of the international oil markets, it's hard to know whether existing crude discounts will persist or future discounts will emerge elsewhere. Consequently, it's also rather difficult to determine whether a refiner's access to cost-advantaged feedstock and the corresponding excess returns are sustainable for 10 or 20 years. For example, early in the development of a new oil source, production may have to be sold at a discount because of a lack of transportation alternatives. In most cases, however, alternatives are usually quick to arrive, causing prices to move toward international benchmarks, and discounts to narrow. As a result, it often takes something more sustainable or predictable than lack of transportation to maintain discounts and deliver moats. For instance, in the case of U.S. refiners that earn narrow economic moats, a government ban on crude oil exports protects these companies' access to discounted crude. Additionally, efficient scale comes into play, as the cost and regulatory approval needed to build new refineries creates a barrier to entry and helps maintain an advantage for all U.S. refiners.

Valero is an example of a refiner with a feedstock advantage that has created a narrow moat. Valero's system of 14 refineries is more complex than competitors', which allows the firm to process lower-quality feedstock into a high-value product. By using cost-advantaged crude or residuals for about two thirds of its feedstock, Valero can take advantage of the discount at which these crudes typically trade compared with light crude. As a result, Valero has historically delivered higher margins than its competitors. Valero is also the biggest exporter among its peers, further strengthening its moat.

Key questions to ask when evaluating refiners:

- Does a refiner have access to cost-advantaged feedstock? Determine whether a refiner can achieve higher margins by processing lower-cost crude through proximity to production, access to stranded crude, or ability to process lower-quality crude.
- Will substantial investment be required for the advantage? By investing in upgrading capacity to process cheaper, lower-quality crude, a refiner's returns will be increasingly dependent on sustained discounts on heavy, sour crude. Without a sufficient uplift in realized margins from the quality discounts, the investment may not earn economic returns. Consequently, a refiner may not be able to generate excess returns to earn a moat.
- Is the refiner's access or cost advantage sustainable? A moat rests on the ability to deliver sustainable excess returns. If a refiner's cost advantage is not sustainable, then a moat is unlikely. Also, market forces may quickly negate any advantage, meaning sustainability may require something that disrupts the market from operating efficiently, such as government regulation.

Oil and Gas Integrateds

For integrated oil and gas companies, which essentially combine the E&P and refining processes, the main source of moat is a resource base that is low cost or economically advantaged (referred to as the upstream part of the process). To a much lesser extent, moat can also result from the firms' refining and chemicals assets (the downstream part of the process), which can benefit from feedstock cost advantages and efficient scale. So, an integrated firm can have a moat based on its upstream or downstream segment (or both), and analyzing moats for these segments of an integrated company is no different than evaluating the moats of independent E&Ps and refiners.

When done properly, integrating the E&P and refining processes can enhance returns on capital and widen moats for integrated firms. Value-added integration can be realized in many ways. For example, integrated firms can leverage the downstream segment's intelligence and capabilities when planning upstream projects to make sure production finds the best markets and realizes the highest prices. Site sharing, particularly between refining and chemical manufacturing, can add value through feedstock flexibility, which ensures that the highest-value product is being produced at any given time and allows byproducts from one operation to be used as feedstock in another. Site sharing also allows for shared services and lower costs.

Integration works best when a firm's upstream and downstream assets are aligned such that one segment can recapture economic rents the other is losing. This scenario is most likely when upstream assets produce the same type and quantity of crude that is processed downstream at the company's refineries. When successful, integration can remove some of the volatility inherent in both the upstream and downstream segments. As a result, returns on capital over the industry cycle are more predictable, which can increase confidence that an integrated firm will generate consistent excess returns in future years, leading to more moats among integrateds than among independent refiners or E&P companies. For us to consider a wide moat, however, we need to see top-quality upstream and downstream assets that are both exceptionally well run. Value created through integration can definitely add to a firm's wide moat, but would never be the sole source if the underlying segments don't have competitive advantages of their own.

Exxon Mobil is an example of an integrated firm that earns our wide moat rating, mostly because it has been able to institutionalize practices that continually deliver superior returns compared with its competitors. Embedded in ExxonMobil's culture is a relentless pursuit of cost savings and operational improvement. As a result, the company can ensure operational continuity throughout its global operations. This allows it to capitalize on worldwide integration of its upstream and downstream segments to drive costs out of the system. Integration, particularly with chemical production, also adds value to its refining operations. Meanwhile, by leveraging its size, the company can achieve economies of scale to contain costs.

Additionally, ExxonMobil centralizes its capital-allocation activities. Consequently, the company evaluates projects from around the world against one another, and only those with the most attractive returns receive funding. With this disciplined approach, the company avoids overinvesting at the height of commodity cycles. Because of the nature of its larger projects, the company must take a long-term approach that prevents it from counting on elevated commodity prices to drive project economics. Instead, the focus is on delivering projects on time and under budget, ensuring that original economics remain in place. Part of the company's moat also owes to its financial strength. Strong cash flow, large cash balances, and low debt levels enable the company to maintain a low cost of capital and to continue investing without relying on capital markets.

Key considerations for evaluating integrateds:

- Can an integrated firm's downstream operations capture value not realized by its upstream? For example, if a company produces oil in a geography where price differentials are significant, are its downstream assets capturing this pricing discount in the form of higher refining/chemicals margins?
- What is the ratio of hydrocarbon production to refining capacity? Are these balanced to the point that the company is truly integrated?
- Is a company utilizing downstream knowledge to optimize its upstream, and vice versa?
- Are refining and chemicals facilities adjacent to each other? Such configurations allow a company to optimize feedstock slates to maximize value.

Engineering Services

Engineering services firms perform and provide the required services and equipment needed to extract commodities from geological deposits. These companies provide the expertise, services, and equipment necessary to solve complex problems in often-challenging operating environments in an efficient and cost-effective manner.

With engineering services firms, we move beyond the cost advantages that are the primary moat sources for many types of energy companies and find other intangible moat sources, such as a reputation for reliability, strong track records of execution, and wide-reaching product portfolios. These sophisticated firms are often asked to solve some of the most difficult engineering problems on the planet while operating in deeply hostile environments, and customers are very reluctant to use unproven providers because a mistake could cost hundreds of millions of dollars. As a result, customers tend to standardize with just a few providers that can meet all of their needs in a variety of situations and geographies, making the engineering services industry rather consolidated, with three or four major providers controlling the bulk of a particular market or product line. As the operating environments are often very dangerous (and can include war zones), safety records are also a factor. Customers do tender for work and break projects up into segments in order to promote competition, but pricing is generally rational because of the industry's oligopolistic structure.

Wide moats are possible in the engineering services industry, more so than with many other types energy firms, thanks to its mix of moat sources: cost advantage, intangible assets, and efficient scale. Companies with near-comprehensive product portfolios that operate with a global manufacturing or engineering base are best positioned to serve customers in a reliable, safe, and efficient manner, making them more likely to earn positions of trust through a history of strong project deliveries. These engineering firms also have the scale required to deploy more funds than their peers do into research efforts and to develop the integrated technologies required—often through collaborating with their customers—to improve future project outcomes. Wide moats can also exist for companies that operate in a small enough market niche where the need to build out the required lab infrastructure, duplicate the decades of research work, and hire the hard-to-find-engineers creates too high a hurdle for new entrants.

Schlumberger holds an industry-leading position in the engineering services arena, bringing it many advantages and earning it a wide moat. The firm's product portfolio is one of the oil services industry's broadest, and its size and reputation give it a nearly unparalleled view into the oilfield complex, allowing it to tackle some of the industry's most difficult and global challenges. In addition, Schlumberger's global base of locally trained engineers helps with its cost structure, lets the firm quickly deploy product lines and talent as needed, and strengthens relationships with countries' national oil companies, which are increasingly some of the firm's most important customers.

Schlumberger's wide moat is driven by its large research and development (R&D) budget, which consistently churns out commercial successes, but is further supported by a clever acquisition strategy, deep international presence, and comprehensive product portfolio. The company focuses on small acquisitions where the software can easily be integrated into its existing product lines, feeding its competitive advantage in R&D. In addition, its deep international presence—for 40 years it has been hiring workers in the countries where it works—and robust product portfolio mean Schlumberger often has better relationships with national oil companies, making it more likely to win high-profile projects.

Key considerations for evaluating engineering services firms:

- How large and how global is the firm relative to peers? A larger and more global firm is likely to earn excess returns on invested capital over a long time frame, increasing our confidence in its competitive advantages.
- What types of engineering issues are being solved? Certain engineering niches have an abundant supply of skilled engineers that apply largely standardized designs to common project requests, which results in very price-competitive markets. Other, more attractive niches involve operating in harsh environments, require custom or fully integrated solutions, and have a shortage of talent.
- How integrated is the company's product portfolio? Companies that provide only a few products are at risk of being made obsolete by competitors with larger product portfolios that can present a fully integrated package with the associated cost and time savings to the customer, locking out peers from winning future work.

12

Financial Services

The financial services sector is all about money, but it's not always the easiest place to make a buck. Money itself, and most financial products, are pure commodities, yet many of the brightest minds in the world—along with a remarkable amount of computing power—are hard at work 24 hours a day trying to outsmart the competition. Add in a generous helping of leverage and it's easy to see why financial companies and their investors have their work cut out for them.

Banking and insurance can be particularly challenging, given largely undifferentiated products and services, regulatory burdens, and a multitude of players vying for a piece of the action. It's just about impossible to convince customers to pay a few extra percentage points for a brand-name car loan, or accept half the going rate on a savings account. Furthermore, macroeconomic factors like interest rates and unemployment contribute to wide swings in profitability. As a result, we rarely see wide moats in either of these industries when there are more than a handful of competitors in a market. Quite a few banks and insurers have been able to dig narrow moats, though, mostly by keeping costs in check.

Percentage of Companies per Rating   Prevalence of Moat Sources (%)

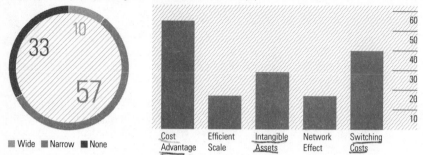

Wide   Narrow   None

Figure 12.1 Economic Moat Characteristics of the Financial Services Sector
SOURCE: Morningstar.

Elsewhere in the sector, economic moats are easier to find. The transactional nature of the financial industry occasionally lends itself to the establishment of powerful network effects. Successful credit card companies and financial exchanges have established moats, thanks to their networks of cardholders, merchants, and traders. We've identified several wide-moat firms in these arenas, and as Figure 12.1 shows, cost advantage is the most prevalent moat source in the overall sector.

Banks

Banks serve as financial intermediaries, transforming the raw materials of deposits and other liabilities into productive assets, usually loans and securities. Banks make money through the spread between their borrowing costs and the yields on their balance-sheet assets, which is a function of the interest-rate and credit risks they assume. They can also make money from charging customers fees for various products and services.

Pricing power is hard to come by in the highly competitive banking business. The costs of borrowing as well as the yields available on investments are usually set by the market, leaving little room for banks to distinguish themselves. What's more, given the wide array of banking choices available to consumers, especially in crowded markets like the United States, it can be hard for banks to exert any real bargaining power. Banks in markets with fewer competitors, such as Canada or the United Kingdom, sometimes have a little more flexibility with pricing. Also, banks with structural advantages, such as large, convenient branch networks or deep customer relationships, can sometimes enhance returns by charging higher fees or offering lower rates on deposits.

Cost advantage is an important source of moat for banks. Because of their relatively limited pricing flexibility, banks must rely more on effective cost control as a means of establishing competitive advantage. Management plays a big role in a bank's ability to achieve and maintain a lower cost structure, so it's important to pay extra attention to management strength when assessing banks. Bank management teams must constantly focus on (1) operating more efficiently than peers; (2) underwriting more effectively; and (3) lowering borrowing costs in order to create excess returns. Even then, it's hard for banks to attain returns well in excess of their costs of capital without taking on excessive risk.

Customer switching costs can also be a moat source for banks. Although switching costs are generally low in absolute terms, the hassle of moving accounts often overrides whatever benefits a customer might receive by switching, especially given the intense price competition and limited opportunity for banks to offer attractive incentives. Banks with deep customer relationships spanning multiple product lines are often able to generate higher-than-average switching costs.

Rarely does a bank achieve a strong enough competitive advantage to guarantee excess returns for an extended period of time, so wide moats are uncommon. But many banks, such as Wells Fargo, have managed to dig narrow moats. The major source of Wells Fargo's moat is its low-cost deposit base. Banks make money by investing customer funds in a variety of loans and securities. The less a bank pays for these funds, the better. Wells Fargo benefits from an exceptionally low cost of funds due to its extensive branch presence, outstanding customer service, and ability to sell multiple products to its customers. This makes it a convenient choice for depositors and increases switching costs. Moreover, this well-managed company has been good at keeping interest expenses in check, minimizing pressure to take on risky loans to boost profitability. This combination of impressive operational expense control and conservative underwriting standards cements its position as a low-cost producer. Finally, the company's solid performance during the financial crisis strengthened the intangible yet valuable asset associated with the Wells Fargo brand name.

In some markets, extensive consolidation and tight regulation have lessened the competitive intensity of the banking industry. Banks in Canada and Australia, for example, can achieve wide moats as a result. In these markets, excessive risk-taking has been successfully curbed by regulators, limiting the cost of bad investments. New entrants are rare because of the regulatory environment, and large existing firms seem content to maintain their substantial market shares. In these geographies, banks maintain a high degree of pricing power over their customers.

Key considerations for banks:

- Does the bank operate in a market with numerous effective competitors, or have a handful of dominant firms established a rational oligopoly?
- Are unusually efficient operations the result of structural advantages, such as economies of scale or an unusual business model, or are low operating costs related mainly to tight-fisted management?
- Are low credit losses the result of a particular lending niche or regulatory status, or are they due only to skillful underwriting?
- Are low funding costs the result of structural advantages, such as a bank's footprint or high switching costs associated with deep customer relationships?
- What is the nature of the bank's assets and liabilities, and the risk associated with them?
- What is the source and amount of noninterest income at the bank, and what is the bank's competitive advantage in these other lines of business?
- Under what regulatory regime does the firm operate?
- How much excess spread (return on equity <minus> cost of equity) is the firm expected to generate?

Capital Markets

Capital-market firms, such as investment banks and brokerages, primarily assist in creating and trading financial securities. They may charge a fee when acting as an agent for a client, or seek to earn a profit when acting as a principal.

Capital-market moats are built on the network effect, intangibles, and cost advantages. In their role as financial intermediaries, investment banks and brokerages connect sellers that wish to raise capital with buyers that seek to invest their capital. The network effect is an important source of competitive advantage across a number of business lines. For underwriting, a company contemplating an equity or debt offering is likely to seek out an investment bank that has access to a large distribution network of interested buy-side and wealth-management clients, as this type of firm would encourage the most competitive bidding process for its security. Likewise, investors (such as buy-side institutions or wealth-management clients) want a relationship with an underwriter in hopes of receiving an allocation of a hot offering. In mergers and acquisitions, a company may look for a financial advisor that has an extensive geographic network of advisors and clients to find a merger partner. For trading, a brokerage with a large network of trading clients gives both buyers and sellers a higher probability of discretely completing large or otherwise hard-to-fill orders and is a source of valuable pricing information.

A strong reputation can create an intangible competitive advantage for capital-market firms. For example, a well-respected investment bank has a greater chance of being selected as a deal's book runner (the underwriter in charge of running the books and assigning portions of the issue to underwriters), allowing it to capture a larger share of a new issue and a greater proportion of the fees. A renowned name also increases the speed and likelihood of gaining a profitable foothold in a new locale or of breaking into another business line, such as a mergers-and-acquisitions advisory firm that begins offering private equity funds.

Cost advantages can also give an edge to certain brokerage business models. Brokerages with a core electronic trading infrastructure and sufficient scale have lower transaction costs than smaller or full-service brokerages. Low transaction costs can create a barrier to entry and competitive pricing flexibility.

Although we believe currently strong investment banks should be able to earn excess returns on capital for 10 years, thus meriting narrow moats, there's generally too much uncertainty in the capital-market business over the 20-year horizon for us to award wide moats. A reputational hit from mispricing underwritten securities can decrease demand from both issuers and investors, and excess profits derived from cost advantages are kept in check by pricing competition and regulation. In addition, while capital-market companies may look financially healthy today, their often-leveraged business models can lead to solvency and liquidity concerns that bring into question their survival in the near term, let alone their ability to generate excess returns for the next 20 years.

Not all capital-market firms are so risky, though. Lazard, for example, has the largest geographic footprint of its independent peers, and a reputation for providing high-quality financial advice to business and government leaders built over more than 150 years. The company advises companies on mergers and acquisitions (M&A) in good times and restructurings during downturns, minimizing its exposure to economic cycles. And the advice business does not require much leverage, further stabilizing the firm's results. The combination of these factors gives us confidence in the company's ability to continue earning economic profits.

Key considerations for capital-market firms:

- Does the company have the capabilities to compete for the largest and most complex capital-market transactions? Can the company compete for cross-border deals?
- Is the company's distribution network or geographic reach materially increasing?
- Are new financial regulations more likely to threaten current business lines or create opportunities?
- How much of the company's business can be executed on an electronic platform?
- Does the company have high market share in a niche?
- Does the company rely on financial leverage to earn above-average returns on capital?
- To what extent does revenue depend on strong principal investment gains or proprietary trading?

Credit Services

As beneficiaries of powerful network effects, credit services firms (think MasterCard or Visa) often possess narrow or wide economic moats. For these companies, which are essentially in the business of connecting payers and payees, a strong network effect depends on widespread acceptance and usage of a payment network. Each additional user creates value for others—a network widely adopted by payers benefits payees who accept it, while a network widely accepted by payees is an attractive alternative for payers.

Cost advantages also contribute to moats in this industry. Companies can benefit from economies of scale because the incremental costs of processing additional transactions are minimal. Intangible assets can also enhance pricing power as a trusted brand is essentially mandatory for companies that handle payments and other money transfers.

Credit card giant Visa dominates the global market for electronic payments. The company primarily earns fees based on both the volume of payments made under the Visa brand and the number of transactions processed through the Visa network. In a world in which the number of digital payment transactions is constantly growing, this wide-moat company should flourish.

Visa's moat stems from its network of cardholders and merchants. In fact, the company is the quintessential example of the network effect in action: Each additional cardholder makes the Visa brand more attractive to merchants, while each new merchant that accepts Visa makes the brand more attractive to cardholders. As the largest global payment network, Visa's ubiquity ensures that it will have a place in consumers' physical—and digital—wallets for years to come. New competitors (and existing competitors, for that matter) will not find it easy to match the extent of Visa's network, contributing to a long-lasting structural advantage for Visa. Visa also benefits from its trusted brand and has spent billions of dollars over many decades on this important intangible asset.

Key considerations for credit services firms:

- Does the network possess a sizable base of customers willing to generate and accept payments using its product?
- Does the network serve a customer base of large, concentrated payers and payees with significant bargaining power, or small, fragmented users?
- Aside from a critical mass of users, does the network provide anything unique to its customers (affluent customers, lower cost, and so on)?
- What kinds of switching costs do customers face? What is the average customer life?
- Payment systems are heavily regulated around the world. Legislation that limits networks' profitability is an ever-present risk.
- What investments (capital expenditures, marketing, incentives) are required to generate additional transaction volume?
- Does the payment system lend to customers or provide other services?

Financial Exchanges

Cost advantages afforded by economies of scale, network effects, and intangible assets are important sources of competitive advantage for financial exchanges—venues for buying and selling financial products such as stocks, futures, and options. First, exchanges deploy trading technology that requires significant investments of financial and human capital, but once these expenditures are made, the costs of additional transactions that pass through an exchange's systems are relatively small. That explains why surges in volume can be so beneficial to an exchange's bottom line, as the additional activity can typically be run on the exchange's existing systems, creating high margins on the incremental revenue. Network effects are also important because liquidity tends to beget additional liquidity. All else being equal, market participants tend to prefer deep and liquid trading systems over shallower systems where liquidity issues could complicate trading. Intangible assets, such as offering trading products that are not easily available to rival markets, can lead to wide moats for certain exchanges.

CME Group, which operates five futures exchanges, is one firm that we believe has established a wide moat. A key source of CME Group's competitive strength is its clearinghouse operation. Positions that are opened at CME exchanges must also be closed through the same exchange, allowing CME to capture all of the trading and clearing volume. This is in contrast to the stock trading business in which shares can be freely traded across multiple venues. We note, however, that because we view the success of its clearing arm as a key differentiating factor for CME Group, we would view any credible threat—regulatory action, for instance—to this clearing/trading business model as a potential blow to CME Group's strategic position, earnings power, and moat.

Key considerations for financial exchanges:

- What proportion of the firm's products is traded on other exchanges?
- How vertically integrated is a given exchange? For example, does it offer clearing, settlement, and custody services?
- Is the exchange a monopoly, and if not, what are the trends in market share and pricing?
- Do clients have an economic interest in supporting new initiatives?

Insurance

Insurers help their customers by converting risk into a known cost. By aggregating exposures, insurers can, ideally, forecast claims with some accuracy and earn a good return without excessive risk. Although the types of risks insurers cover vary widely, from death to hurricanes, the basic dynamics of the industry are fairly consistent. And although insurance is a somewhat complicated enterprise, it is at its core a commodity business.

Despite the commodity aspects of the industry, insurers can build moats by maintaining a sustainable cost advantage in underwriting, and there are actually multiple ways for insurers to do this. First, an insurer can gain an edge by focusing on less competitive areas of the market. Surplus and excess lines, for instance, are more specialized and less regulated than many other types of insurance, which can boost a firm's flexibility and pricing power. However, operating in these areas will not lead to excess returns unless the company also has the underwriting acumen to properly price policies, and the proper incentives to induce underwriters to avoid poorly priced policies.

Alternatively, insurance companies can look to lower administrative expenses. The most obvious way is to develop the business to take advantage of economies of scale, but there are a few reasons why this strategy has limitations in the insurance industry. For one, the U.S. insurance industry is regulated at the state level, leaving a national insurer with many duplicative costs across states. More important, only a relatively small percentage of insurance costs are fixed. That said, there are still some companies that are able to effectively scale their operations. Personal lines insurance, in particular, is more scalable as it requires fewer specialized underwriters and less human capital. However, we're quick to distinguish between focused scale in a certain aspect of the business and sheer, perhaps sprawling, size. We typically don't believe large, diversified insurers have moats.

There are other ways to reduce costs beyond scale. Companies can lower customer acquisition costs by developing unique and effective distribution platforms. An insurer can also reduce expenses by making customers stickier, as the cost to acquire new policies is much higher than the cost of renewing existing policies. Insurance companies can create stickiness by maintaining a captive agent network or cross-selling multiple policy types. However, these strategies impose additional costs, so a close look is necessary to see if the strategy is effective over time.

As of this writing, no pure insurance companies earn wide moats, and we doubt they ever will. Although insurers can develop a sustainable competitive edge as outlined above, economic moats in insurance are somewhat fragile for a few reasons. First, insurers are exposed to substantial investment risk through the large portfolios they carry, and investment losses can drive returns below the required level even if the insurance operations are performing well. Further, an underwriting advantage can be relatively easily diminished by poor decisions on management's part, either through mispricing risk or expanding into less attractive business areas. Finally, leveraged balance sheets are fundamental to the business model, which can magnify the negative impact of any mistakes or unforeseen losses.

Key considerations for insurers:

- In general, insurers do not benefit from favorable competitive positions. Customers won't pay a meaningful premium for brand and products that are easily replicable, making cost structure the key differentiator.
- Many insurers do not know their cost of goods sold for a number of years, which can result in their underpricing policies without knowing it. Firms have an incentive to chase growth at the expense of long-term profitability and can be forced to match low prices or risk losing business.
- Insurers have two main sources of profitability, underwriting income (premiums minus operating costs) and float income. In our view, superior underwriting income is the only true source of a moat. We do not believe that insurers can gain a sustainable advantage solely through investing, as higher returns are typically reflective of higher risk.
- Insurers need to be evaluated over long periods, as cost volatility is inherent to the industry.
- We view life insurance as less moaty than property/casualty insurance. It is difficult for life insurers to differentiate themselves in underwriting, as mortality rates are relatively consistent, and life insurers are more exposed to capital-market conditions.

13

Healthcare

Despite the many changes and challenges facing the healthcare industry in the 21st century, the sector remains relatively fertile territory for economic moats. Of the roughly 140 healthcare companies Morningstar covers, more than 70% of them have moats, with more than a quarter of those earning our wide moat rating.

Intangible assets can claim much of the credit for the sector's rich moat landscape. Pharmaceutical and biotech companies enjoy long-term patent protection, along with the associated pricing power, for the new drugs they bring to market. Intellectual property and patents are important moat sources for medical device makers as well.

Beyond the magic of patents, several other moat sources exist in the healthcare sector, as Figure 13.1 shows. Cost advantage plays a role for some companies, such as biotech firms with complex processes that are profitable only at large scale. Switching costs are also at work for some companies, particularly those with complicated products that medical professionals are loath to abandon after investing time and energy in learning to use them.

Why Moats Matter

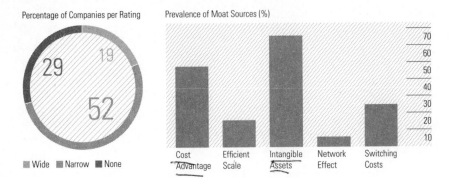

Percentage of Companies per Rating

Prevalence of Moat Sources (%)

29 · 19 · 52

■ Wide ■ Narrow ■ None

Cost Advantage · Efficient Scale · Intangible Assets · Network Effect · Switching Costs

Figure 13.1 Economic Moat Characteristics of the Healthcare Sector
SOURCE: Morningstar.

Pharmaceuticals

Large pharmaceutical companies are in the business of creating, developing, patenting, and marketing drugs worldwide. Often generating robust cash flows from patent-protected drug sales, pharmaceutical firms are usually well positioned to redeploy capital in creating new drugs to launch into their established distribution networks. As a result, all of the major drug manufacturers we cover have moats—most of them wide.

Patents, which generally last for 20 years in the drug industry, are definitely the most important source of moat for these companies. Although some of the exclusivity period passes during a drug's development time, once a drug is approved, drug companies can charge monopolistic prices. Since drug sales fall by roughly 90% after a patent expires in a developed market, companies must continually offset generic competition with new patented product launches in order to sustain their moats. In emerging markets, however, brand names are more important than patents, enabling drugs to maintain market share in these regions well after the exclusivity period ends.

Outside of patents, other moat sources can add further support for some large diversified pharmaceutical companies. Brand power exists not only in emerging markets, but also in consumer and animal drug products, where consumers are willing to pay more for trusted brands. Efficient scale tends to support rare-disease drugs, where very small populations reduce the incentive for new entrants.

The difference between a wide moat and a narrow one in the pharmaceuticals business depends largely on the diversity of products that are generating

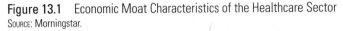

the majority of a firm's sales. The more drugs a company sells in multiple regions of the world, the greater the likelihood that it will be able to create new drugs to sustain high returns on invested capital. Further, the diversity of drugs also increases the likelihood that the firm can sustain new branded competitive threats and emerging side effects, two of the most likely negative events that can cut off high returns from a drug before the patent protection ends. Additionally, a high diversity of drugs tends to further entrench distribution and manufacturing capabilities, which increases the odds of a partnership with a smaller innovative firm to bring an externally created drug to the market.

Among the major pharmaceutical companies, giant Johnson & Johnson carries one of the widest moats, thanks to a diverse revenue base, a robust research pipeline, and exceptional cash-flow generation. In fact, we believe Johnson & Johnson stands alone as a leader across the major healthcare industries and probably has the widest moat of any company in the entire broad healthcare sector.

Johnson & Johnson's diverse operations support the company's wide moat. The company holds a leadership role in a number of segments, including medical devices, over-the-counter medicines, and several pharmaceutical markets. The company is not overly dependent on one particular operating segment, and within each segment, no one product dominates sales, like Pfizer's Lipitor did. Despite carrying some lower-margin divisions, the company maintains strong pricing power and has posted gross margins approaching 70% during the past five years, validating its strong competitive position.

Johnson & Johnson has a number of other things going for it as well. Thanks to its strong research and development, or R&D, program, J&J is poised to launch several potential blockbusters during the next few years, which should allow the company to escape largely unscathed from big patent expirations, unlike many of its competitors. Its efforts in medical devices, including ceramic orthopedics and minimally invasive surgical tools, should help maintain leadership in several medical-device groups as well as support strong pricing power. J&J's powerful salesforce should continue to make the company a partner of choice for smaller healthcare companies that are developing new products. Further, the firm's hands-off style for recently acquired companies may also entice companies with innovative products to become part of this conglomerate, allowing Johnson & Johnson to maintain its status as the largest and most profitable healthcare company in the world.

Key considerations when researching large pharmaceuticals:

- How strong is the company's ability to develop new medicines to replace drugs losing patent protection? Combining the impact of patent losses and probability-adjusted sales forecasts for new product launches sets a good proxy to determine the company's ability to offset generic competition. Qualitatively, past rates of successful drug development also tend to influence the probability of new drug approvals.
- Given the importance of regulatory agencies in approving and reimbursing new drugs, how are governments embracing and paying for new drug innovation? Also, although government payers are important worldwide, large consolidated private payers in the U.S. and individual private payers in emerging markets are also critical.
- What percentage of sales is derived from hard-to-make drugs? Biologics and vaccines not only have patent protection, but the difficulty in manufacturing, marketing, and gaining regulatory approval for these drugs also creates additional barriers to entry for competitors.
- If the company operates outside the traditional drug businesses, how strong are its competitive advantages in those areas? For example, animal-health drugs, consumer products, vaccines, generics, and emerging markets potentially contain barriers to entry that are unique from human pharmaceutical drugs.

Biotechnology

Biotechnology firms are typically smaller, more innovative, riskier versions of big pharmaceutical firms. They generally seek to discover new therapies using biologic rather than chemical processes, though today's pharmaceutical firms frequently employ both methods. Biotechs tend to fall into three categories: established, emerging, and speculative, with moats residing mainly in the first two.

We see three key sources of moats in this industry: intangible assets, efficient scale, and cost advantages. First, intangible assets are crucial and can come in many forms. Barriers to entry are the most important intangible assets for biotechs; these barriers typically stem from patent strength, patent duration, and the complexity of the molecules in the firm's portfolio. The broader competitive dynamics of a given therapeutic area can also make it more or less conducive to establishing sustainable, strong profit streams. For example, R&D efforts are shifting away from primary-care treatments and toward severe diseases with few treatment options, where pricing power is strong and sales requirements are lower. The breadth of a firm's portfolio can be an indicator of the strength of intangible assets such as R&D productivity or business development success; breadth also provides a buffer against increased competitive threats to a single product.

The strongest moats are typically built on efficient scale, and we believe a few rare-disease-focused firms, such as BioMarin and Alexion, possess this competitive advantage. These firms focus on markets that are best served by only one or a very small number of players, as competition is discouraged by high initial costs (identifying and locating small target-patient populations) and smaller payouts (small number of patients served globally). A company with a first-mover advantage could enjoy exorbitant profit margins, minimal pushback from payers and regulators, and minimal competitive threats.

Some markets that require complex biologics manufacturing processes are profitable only at a large scale, creating a cost advantage for some firms. For example, while plasma collection, fractionation, and processing could be cost prohibitive if a firm had only one resulting marketed product, successful companies are able to efficiently convert plasma into several marketed products. Expensive and complex manufacturing requirements have limited this market to a handful of experienced global industry players, such as Baxter and Grifols.

For biotechs, patent quality, portfolio strength, and R&D strategy determine whether moats are narrow or wide. Brand-name drugs enjoy patent protection for 20 years, but because a patent application is usually filed as soon as a drug is identified, drugs rarely enjoy 20 years of monopoly profits, as a significant portion of the protected period is eaten up by the trials. Many drugs enjoy only eight to 10 years of patent protection after they're launched in the marketplace, so it is crucial to explicitly identify the exclusivity life of each drug when assigning moats. Highly complex drugs can be difficult to re-create even after patent expiration, which can add durability to a moat. Depending on a molecule's position on the complexity spectrum, barriers to entry may become insurmountable for the competition. Drugs targeting an unmet need are more likely to support moats, and orphan drug status—a designation for drugs developed specifically to treat rare medical conditions—enhances a drug's shelf life. When combined with strong diversification and R&D strategies that look replicable, these qualities can add a layer of protection to returns on capital and can push some biotechs, such as Amgen, Novo Nordisk, and Roche Holding, into the wide-moat category.

Key considerations for biotech companies:

- Do existing patents give the firm's drugs adequate protection during the next 10 years? How strong are these patents (process versus composition)?
- How susceptible is the company's drug portfolio to generic competition? What is the drug's location on the complexity curve? Can generic companies easily replicate the manufacturing and (if necessary) clinical-trials processes?
- How attractive is the therapeutic area? Assess the size of the marketplace, as well as the regulatory and reimbursement landscape, and identify the likely number of current and future competitors. Determine whether barriers to entry are low or high based on the therapeutic area's attributes.
- How productive is the firm's R&D? Are R&D investments sufficient to maintain the firm's competitive advantages? Assess the productivity and strength of its development platform and its ability to produce new candidates.

Medical Devices

Medical-device companies make temporary and permanently implantable hardware for the human body, such as pacemakers and artificial hips, and we believe economic moats are plentiful in the industry. As with other healthcare firms, intellectual property, regulatory requirements, switching costs, and physician relationships all keep new entrants at bay in this sector. These barriers are usually enough to maintain medical-device moats, but established competitors can also use their cash-rich balance sheets to scoop up new entrants that become viable threats to their oligopolistic industry structure.

Intangible assets, including intellectual property and relationships with healthcare professionals, are one primary source of economic moat for medical-device companies. These companies often create slightly differentiated products that are not necessarily interchangeable, thanks to patent protection. These firms will often engage in aggressive defense of their intellectual property, and there is typically a low level of ongoing litigation between rivals that continues even years after that generation of products has become obsolete. Moats are also derived from close relationships with medical practitioners and sales representatives, who are highly trained on this specialized equipment. These service reps often provide advice in the operating room, which is especially valued by the majority of physicians whose practices do not see high patient volume. Among orthopedic companies, moats stem from high switching costs that often keep surgeons wedded to one company's implants and tools for years. Among cardiac companies, efficient scale is another key component to moats; there are only three primary competitors that have captured roughly 90% of the market, so they operate as a rational oligopoly.

Device makers with wide moats consist only of those that have the most differentiated (and least substitutable) products, and the most practitioners locked in with high switching costs. Some products, by their nature, are more interchangeable than others, such as coronary stents made by Boston Scientific and Abbott. For companies like these that rely heavily on products with low switching costs, we generally award narrow moats. Narrow-moat companies may also be device firms that rely on a smaller range of products, which leaves them more vulnerable to any disruptive technology. In contrast, wide-moat companies sell a broader product portfolio with greater proportions of less-interchangeable products. Medtronic is a good example of a wide-moat device maker, as its spine products benefit from high switching costs associated with the steep and lengthy learning curve that surgeons must climb, and its cardiac rhythm management devices are only modestly vulnerable to substitutes.

Other considerations for medical device makers:

- Is the company pioneering any emerging technologies? Look for novel technologies in the pipeline, especially those that will address untreated or undertreated patient populations. Additionally, examine whether any pipeline products will offer significantly improved clinical outcomes or procedure success.
- When assessing the competitive landscape, we typically include the drug manufacturers because there can be innovations in medical therapy that end up competing with device therapies. This happens most frequently with cardiac device makers.
- Device makers often depend on serial acquisition to complement internal efforts at innovation. Because of the danger of overpaying for purchases,

we like to look at returns on invested capital, or ROICs, that include good-will, as this measure more accurately reflects all investments made on an ongoing basis.

- What does the reimbursement picture look like? For some device makers, establishing reimbursement is critical to product success. The Centers for Medicare and Medicaid serve as a bellwether that often sets the benchmark for private payers. Well-designed trials and favorable clinical outcomes that significantly exceed existing therapies are critical to gaining the coopera-tion of payers.

Medical Instruments and Supplies

Medical instruments and supplies companies make instrumentation used for hospital procedures as well as basic supplies used by both healthcare provid-ers and individual customers. The most common moat source for the instruments and supplies industry has been high switching costs. Surgeons require train-ing on specific, complicated instruments, making them hesitant to switch to less familiar products even if they are cheaper. Barriers to entry are also gen-erally high given the sizable initial investment required to build manufacturing and distribution infrastructure. Having a sizable scale and scope advantage gives larger entrenched players the ability to maintain pricing power and market share in more commoditized product lines, while making new rising players with valuable products into acquisition targets. R&D expertise can also strengthen a moat, as superior features or proven effectiveness versus competitors allows firms to maintain their competitive positioning and flex their pricing muscle.

In order to achieve wide moats in this industry, companies need to either be focused on areas of unmet needs or have rational oligopolies. The switching-cost factor is weakening somewhat in today's environment because buying decisions are shifting from the hands of practitioners to administrators, as strained hospital budgets and a broad focus on reimbursement cuts are reducing the instrument makers' power over their customers. Competition is intensify-ing in commoditized products, so to warrant wide moats, firms have to either focus on areas of unmet needs with highly differentiated products (such as robotic surgery, the specialty of wide-moat Intuitive Surgical) or dominate oli-gopolistic niches, such as minimally invasive surgery instrumentation, where practitioners' inertia and the absence of irrational competition result in stable market shares.

Other considerations for medical instruments and supplies companies:

- How commoditized are the company's product lines? If the firm mainly competes in undifferentiated areas, does it have cost advantages or other factors that still allow it to generate superior returns?
- How attractive is the surgical area? Assess the size of the marketplace and the pace of technological change, evaluate the regulatory and reimbursement landscape, and identify the likely number of current and future competitors. Determine whether barriers to entry are high based on this area's attributes.
- Technological superiority by itself is almost never a sustainable source of a moat, but coupled with other factors, such as a razor/razor-blade operating model or massive distribution infrastructure, it becomes powerful. The marketplace for devices targeting unmet needs could be particularly lucrative, as the regulatory and reimbursement environment tends to be fairly favorable, allowing greater and more durable excess returns.
- Instrument makers frequently supplement internal R&D efforts with acquisitions, both to enter new therapeutic areas and to fend off new competitors. Capitalizing R&D or adjusting goodwill for acquisitions is important when comparing returns on capital for companies across the space.

Diagnostics and Research

The diagnostics and research industry includes firms that sell products or services that aid in the drug-development or diagnostic process. This includes equipment and consumables manufacturers and distributors, clinical research organizations, and diagnostic laboratories.

Switching costs are the most powerful competitive advantage in the diagnostics and research industry. Firms with economic moats in this industry typically benefit from high switching costs, either in the form of large required up-front investments or a significant time commitment. Razor-and-blade firms, such as Waters or Agilent, lock in customers that are unlikely to switch to a competitor's product, given the significant up-front investment it would require. These firms also tend to focus on product lines that require extensive training for end users. Once customers are trained and have experience in a certain product, they are hesitant to switch. Being involved with drug research provides an extra layer of protection for the incumbents, as a pharmaceutical or biotech firm would need to revalidate clinical trial data in order to make any changes to the manufacturing process for its drugs.

The industry also benefits from intangible assets and cost advantages. Products enjoy patent protection, but the range of this protection varies based on the sophistication level of the product. For most product lines, technology on its own offers very little defense against new entrants. In the clinical research organization industry, top-tier firms benefit from expertise, knowledge, and powerful data that can set them apart from weaker competitors and warrant premium pricing. Cost advantage can play a small role, specifically in lower-end commodified product categories, but in the higher-end equipment markets, price is not typically the primary driver of purchase decisions. Customers are willing to pay up for better or more convenient products. In the reference lab business, scale is critical. The largest players, LabCorp and Quest, essentially form a duopoly, as high volume allows them to efficiently process lab tests at lower costs than smaller competitors can. Finally, while rare, efficient scale could also contribute to a moat if a product niche is small yet lucrative enough for only a few players.

Other considerations when researching diagnostics and research firms:

- How sticky is the customer base? Firms selling instrumentation that requires extensive training tend to have stickier customers because clients are reluctant to switch to a competitor's product and be retrained. If the firm's products are used throughout the clinical research process, how critical is the company's product to the process? Would a switch to a competitor's platform require the researcher to obtain clearances from the various regulatory agencies?
- Does the firm benefit from the razor-and-blade model, with switching costs that are typically higher? How much of the total revenue is attributable to a recurring component (consumables and services) versus capital equipment?
- How sophisticated are the firm's products? Firms with complex products are more likely to fend off competition for a longer time and probably possess technological expertise that can be applied to next-generation products. A focus on low-tech products typically exposes firms to competition from low-cost manufacturers that will attempt to undercut on price. Gross margins are key indicators when comparing products from a technological perspective.

14

Industrials

The industrials sector is a hodgepodge. It's an eclectic group of companies spanning a wide range of industries with varying characteristics and potential moat sources. As such, it's difficult to generalize about moat sources, and we see a little bit of everything in this broad sector. In this chapter, we have selected just a few industries that we think are representative of how companies can establish moats, but given the breadth of industries in this sector, we don't touch on every type of industrial firm.

Efficient scale, for example, is an important moat source for airport and marine-port operators as well as for railroads, given these businesses' natural geographic monopoly positions and the limited number of facilities needed in any one market. Intangible assets are also a factor for many industrials. For airport operators, intangible assets come in the form of operating rights granted by the government, a prize usually won after years and years of relationship-building with the powers that be. Relationships are important in the aerospace and defense industry, too, where the most valuable intangible asset is familiarity

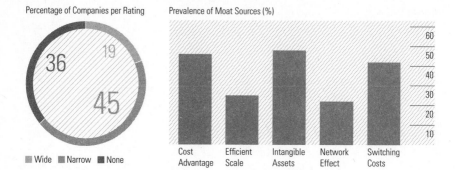

Percentage of Companies per Rating   Prevalence of Moat Sources (%)

■ Wide ■ Narrow ■ None

Figure 14.1   Economic Moat Characteristics of the Industrials Sector
SOURCE: Morningstar.

with the complex workings of government customers. Switching costs also matter a lot in aerospace and defense, given the sophisticated technologies and significant training requirements. Cost advantage is a key driver for railroads, which can move freight more cheaply than many other transport options. And network effect helps heavy equipment companies that rely on broad dealer networks to service their equipment quickly and effectively in the field.

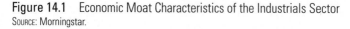

The moatiest subindustry in this sector is diversified industrials—holding companies that can build moat by leveraging core competencies across multiple platforms. Least moaty is the trucking industry, where it's difficult to gain competitive advantage through cost advantages, network effect, switching costs, or intangibles such as brand. Figure 14.1 gives a look at the distribution of moat ratings and sources in the industrials sector.

Railroads

Railroads haul coal, chemicals, grain, intermodal containers, automobiles, lumber, crude oil, and other commodities. Railroads in North America, unlike those in many other regions, generally own the real estate or rights-of-way, track, and terminals over which they operate, as well as the engines and cars.

Railroads earn their wide economic moats from cost advantage and efficient scale. Although other transportation modes like barges, aircraft, and trucks also haul freight, railroads are by far the lowest-cost option when no waterway connects the origin and destination. Railroads are also 4 times more fuel-efficient than trucks, and long freight trains make more effective use of manpower despite their need for train-yard personnel. Even for products that can be shipped by truck, railroads charge customers 10% to 30% less than truckers to transport containers between the same origin and destination.

Railroads also operate at efficient scale. For all but the busiest lanes (like Wyoming's coal-rich Powder River Basin), a single railroad generally serves an end-of-the-line shipper, and only two railroads operate per region in North America. Barriers to entry help railroad companies, too; the need to obtain contiguous rights-of-way on which to lay continuously welded steel rail spanning a significant portion of a huge continent fends off would-be entrants in North America. Railroads may build new spurs or restore abandoned lines, but we doubt any new mainlines will be built.

Key to railroad moats is pricing that is adequate to cover costs including required reinvestments. In this area, the rails are acting more rationally than in the past, as the attitude of "lose money on every car, but make it up on volume" has gone the way of the dinosaur in an era of modern management. Industry consolidation has facilitated rationality; North America had more than 40 Class I rails in 1980, while today there are just seven. However, unlike trucks or barges, railroads must maintain their own roads, and resulting heavy capital-expense requirements (annually 16%–20% of revenue) temper free cash flow. When considering railroads outside of North America, we'd look for similar pricing power and government interest in maintaining viable private rail transportation.

Other important considerations for railroads:

- Increasingly efficient use of labor and fuel are fertile areas for operational improvement. How are the rails continuing to advance in both aspects of margin improvement?
- Shippers consistently lobby to decrease railroad pricing power. Does the legislative and regulatory environment threaten to undo profitable pricing?
- Capital investment dwarfs depreciation. We believe deferred tax liabilities will persist because of different depreciation methods used in filing SEC reports and taxes, so we project that cash tax will be in line with historical cash tax rates and lower than income-statement tax rates.
- Unfunded government mandates like precision train control could cost the railroads billions of dollars, and yield no economic benefit. This cash flow would otherwise benefit investors.

Airport Operators

Although most airports around the world are owned by government authorities, private operators often manage all the workings of the airport—everything from runway maintenance to food service and more. Most of these private companies are granted operating rights that last multiple decades.

For airport operators, intangible assets and efficient scale are the keys to moat creation. Acquiring the rights from the government to operate and manage the airport is the most important source of moat. This requires prior experience and relationships with politicians. New entrants need to convince regulatory authorities that new infrastructure would be beneficial to the country or area in some fashion. All operators are required to set and execute long-term (five- to 10-year) development plans that include proposed improvements and enhancements to the airports, lending a degree of certainty to what the future may hold. Furthermore, efficient scale is at play in this area because having too many airports in a market would reduce profits for all parties.

To determine moat width in this area, we look at the duration of a company's operating rights, as well as the impact of regulation on pricing. Most operators are generally given decades-long rights to operate and manage the airports. In Mexico, operators received generous 50-year rights starting in 1999, leading us to award wide moat ratings to Mexican companies such as Grupo Aeroportuario del Sureste. However, some governments do not allow operators to earn significant excess returns on capital, treating the airport like a regulated utility rather than a private business. This is the case for Aéroports de Paris, which has no moat despite its monopolylike status.

Key considerations for airports and air services:

- What is the bidding process for granting rights to manage and operate the airport?
- What is the duration of the operating contract?
- Does the government allow the operator to earn a return in excess of the cost of capital?
- What level of traffic moves through the airport?
- How much capital investment is required, and do operators have the power to raise prices to cover increases in fixed and variable costs?
- Does the operator have the opportunity to grow through acquisitions in other geographically advantaged areas?

Aerospace and Defense

Aerospace and defense firms design, engineer, manufacture, and manage supply chains for the production and sale of advanced equipment including fighter and cargo aircraft, land vehicles, water-based destroyers and submarines, and missiles and munitions. Worldwide customers are often governments but also include commercial clients.

Familiarity with the complex workings of government customers is the most important source of intangible assets for defense companies. Successful firms build this knowledge through decades of interactions and relationship building, making it difficult for new entrants to catch up. Switching costs deliver another advantage, as the significant training required to use and maintain new equipment offers incumbent providers an advantage. The armed forces have hundreds of thousands of people who need to perform for mission success, and new equipment creates a cost of readiness. What's more, new equipment is scrutinized by all levels of the government, ranging from those who use it to those who pay for it.

Thanks to the industry's complexity and very high switching costs, narrow moats are quite common. Only two companies—Lockheed Martin and General Dynamics—have garnered wide moat ratings, thanks to dominance in military aircraft and limited competition for naval vessels, respectively. Other firms like Boeing enjoy high barriers to entry, but fierce competition for market share and an unprofitable customer base for commercial aircraft (with lead airlines canceling orders) limit the certainty of excess returns and keep moats narrow.

Other considerations for aerospace and defense:

- Can a new entrant effectively compete against the five dominant defense providers in the U.S. market? Does the company have a niche that will allow a healthy return on capital? The U.S. defense industry consolidated to five players from 50 in the 1990s, and each player has well-diversified platforms and programs.
- Does the defense contractor understand the mechanics of bidding and winning business? Arcane government regulations that have been built over decades outline the sales process, including the accounting and patent controls, and have the effect of restricting new entrants.
- Are existing returns on capital strong because of lower cost of manufacturing infrastructure or because of governments' perceived needs of a healthy

industrial base? Can they withstand lower switching costs and more competitive bidding?

- Can a new commercial aircraft manufacturer attain regulatory approval from governments in various jurisdictions? Can it effectively manage the multitude of suppliers needed to build the plane? Healthy returns on capital in the aerospace industry are driven by negative working capital as customers make payments ahead of aircraft delivery, and shouldn't be used as a sole metric to support presence of a moat.

Trucking and Marine Shipping

Truckload carriers move full trailer loads for individual shippers, while less-than-truckload, or LTL, firms consolidate and move smaller loads from multiple customers. In the marine segment, inland tank-barge providers move bulk liquid cargo throughout the domestic U.S. inland waterway system, while the large steamship lines concentrate on shipping containerized ocean freight.

Trucking is a difficult business in which to construct an economic moat. In fact, we currently give no-moat ratings to all of the pure-play truckload and LTL firms we cover. We don't see much opportunity for a carrier to establish a competitive advantage via the network effect, switching costs, or brand identity. At first glance, it might seem that high fixed costs (equipment fleets and driver wages) should allow for cost advantages through superior processes or scale economies, but those have proven insufficiently sustainable. In the truckload industry, there are low switching costs and few barriers to entry—one need only purchase a single truck to haul customers' freight. In LTL shipping, which is more capital intensive and concentrated than the truckload segment, given the need for a broad network of consolidation terminals, economies of scale have fallen short. Even the largest domestic LTL carriers can face near-bankruptcy during a severe freight recession as competitors slash rates to unsustainable levels in an attempt to keep trucks loaded.

Moats are also uncommon in the global marine shipping market, given high capital intensity and low switching costs. These factors drive high cyclicality and intense price competition. Even the largest ocean liners remain price takers, and profitability has suffered across the industry thanks to persistent oversupply.

Kirby Corp., the largest tank-barge operator in the U.S., is an exception. We think efficiencies and cost advantages from scale economies provide Kirby with a narrow economic moat capable of defending long-run profitability from competing tank-barge operators. Through a combination of acquisitions and some organic growth, Kirby has amassed the largest fleet in the inland and coastwise tank-barging industry—twice that of its next largest competitor, American Commercial Lines. This kind of scale, which would be difficult and costly to replicate, allows the firm to reposition barges more quickly than many of its competitors can, while capitalizing on additional backhaul opportunities, all of which increase utilization. Furthermore, the firm's vast fleet footprint increases the likelihood it will have the right kind of barge available for different kinds of cargo. That is, the company can avoid changing cargo on a given barge, which often involves expensive cleaning methods that increase transportation costs (particularly for petrochemicals). Additionally, Kirby's barging business enjoys protection from foreign competition thanks to the Jones Act, which restricts U.S. marine shipping to domestically owned carriers.

Key considerations for trucking and marine shipping:

- Trucking and containerized ocean transport are asset-intensive businesses with high levels of fixed costs (equipment is expensive) and few opportunities to differentiate. Consequently, moatworthy operations are few and far between.
- For truckload and LTL carriers, significant deterioration in pricing power and irrational rate-setting (often measured by changes in rate per mile) during periods of sluggish freight demand are key signs of a commoditized operation marked by asset intensity and limited switching costs.
- In the domestic inland tank-barging business, significant network scale can bestow superior operating efficiencies in terms of lower costs (fewer empty miles) and better service (widespread availability of specialized equipment). U.S. domestic marine shippers are also protected from foreign operators via government regulation (per the Merchant Marine Act of 1920, also known as the Jones Act).
- Marine port operators are often able to build moats through efficient scale, as few regions globally can justify the presence of several competitors.

Waste Management

Integrated waste-management companies establish collection routes around a network of physical assets, such as landfills, incinerators, and recycling centers.

Nonhazardous-waste vendors handle the majority of trash generated by munici-pal, industrial, and commercial customers. Hazardous-waste companies are subject to greater regulation and often handle specific types of waste, such as medical or radioactive.

In the waste-management industry, vertical integration (where one firm controls multiple aspects of a process) is an important competitive advantage that leads to pricing power and operational efficiency. Owners of landfills or incinerator sites often have regulatory permits that give them exclusive rights to operate disposal facilities for 10 to 20 years, allowing them to set the price or "tipping fee" for the privilege of dumping waste at these regulated sites. However, the capital intensity of the waste industry also requires disposal asset owners to attract sufficient volumes to their facilities if they want to be profit-able. Vertically integrated waste companies that handle collection and disposal can offer customers a bundled price for both services, which can lead to greater volumes of waste funneled through company-owned disposal assets. This ver-tical integration supports efficient scale, which ultimately discourages new entrants from attempting to break into an established waste market.

Route density can be another type of advantage for waste collectors. Each new stop on a collection route represents additional volume at a marginal cost. In aggregate, excess free cash flow generated by a network of dense collection routes can be reinvested back into operational improvements to increase efficiency.

In hazardous waste, we believe the risk of unreliable service increases switching costs, as ultimate environmental liability remains with the waste generator. Because of this, customers are more inclined to stick with proven vendors that demonstrate reliable track records. Vertical integration minimizes the number of vendors and creates closed-loop systems, which can diminish the risk of an adverse environmental event.

A number of vertically integrated waste operators have turned these com-petitive advantages into narrow economic moats, but thus far, only medical-waste specialist Stericycle has managed a wide moat. Stericycle built its unmatched scale in medical-waste disposal gradually through a series of acquisitions, securing valuable medical waste disposal permits and customer relationships much more quickly than organic development would have allowed. As a result, the company has a dense and hard-to-replicate network of collec-tion routes and processing facilities that navigate a complicated maze of local, state, and federal EPA regulations. Costly permit requirements also discourage new entrants, leaving healthcare institutions with a limited pool of vendors, no viable substitutes for medical-waste processing, and little bargaining power. Stericycle's capacity for efficiently and reliably handling the entire medical-waste stream—from collection to sterilization and incineration—also helps customers minimize risk. In addition, Stericycle benefits from efficient scale in this niche industry. All told, we expect Stericycle to continue producing outsize returns well into the future.

Other considerations for waste management:

- Landfill or incinerator ownership can be a competitive advantage in countries with strict waste-handling regulations. Community opposition and political pressures lengthen the permitting process for new disposal sites, making it difficult for new entrants to replicate or compete against an existing network of established assets.
- Owning disposal capacity leads to pricing power in the industry, which provides the foundation for predictable, annuity-type cash flows.
- Collection routes are often designed to funnel the maximum quantity of waste volumes toward company-owned assets, a metric known as the internalization rate. We believe that vertically integrated operators with high internalization rates (in the neighborhood of 65%) have a greater ability to weather economic downturns than less efficient peers do.
- Although a high degree of operating leverage implies that operating profitability has some economic sensitivity, the necessity of waste handling provides some assurance for a basic level of demand throughout the economic cycle.
- In highly populated areas where land is at a premium, recycling may grow in favor. However, landfill alternatives rarely achieve critical mass without some form of governmental support.

Heavy Equipment

Heavy-equipment firms manufacture value-added finished products for on-road trucking, construction, agriculture, and mining end markets. It is not uncommon for these companies to outsource some or all of their necessary metal fabrication and componentry (such as tires and electronics), and sales are typically either direct to end users or through third-party distribution.

In the heavy-equipment industry, a solid service reputation is critical for moat building; downtime on roads, at project sites, or at mines equates to lost revenue for customers. Whether through a separate dealer network or direct to customers, companies in this industry must support their in-field products with aftermarket parts and servicing. Those in the market with the widest breadth of support and highest quality of service can usually charge premium prices and enjoy better profitability.

In the truck manufacturing business, we believe original-equipment manufacturers, or OEMs—firms that create products for other firms to sell under their own brand names—operate rationally, and price increases tend to occur uniformly when new emissions standards emerge. New entrants have a hard time breaking into this market, and we think this oligopoly will remain intact given strong intangible assets such as customer preferences and product reputation. That said, companies in this industry can separate themselves through low-cost practices and vertical integration in areas such as engine technologies.

Healthy R&D spending is also a good sign for heavy-equipment manufacturers, as new product development can drive better relative growth, premium pricing, and stickier customers. Companies able to consistently fund research can pick up market share during downturns.

Wide-moat firm Caterpillar is the largest heavy-equipment manufacturer in the world and holds a dominant share in the U.S. market. The firm's service network has helped it expand its market share; preventing machine downtime is critical for Caterpillar's customers, so the company's wide dealer network creates a sizable competitive advantage. Caterpillar also enjoys economies of scale as the largest equipment manufacturer in the industry. The company's geographic breadth and strong reputation provide a perceived product advantage that leads to higher-priced equipment and better resale values over time. The firm is unlikely to concede this advantage, as its R&D budget dwarfs competitors' spending.

Key considerations for heavy equipment:

- Distribution networks can provide competitive advantages. The number of dealers is important, but so is quality. Where available, it's appropriate to analyze dealer turnover and financial health.
- Aftermarket sales lead to more-stable operations and stickier customers. A high degree of service revenue can lead to better sustainability and wider

profitability over the entire cycle. Some firms earn more than half of their revenue from this source.

- We recommend capitalizing R&D expenses in return on invested capital, or ROIC, calculations, as they are core investments in the business. In addition, we don't like to see prolonged cuts in this line item for cost-saving purposes.

Diversified Industrials

For diversified industrial firms, which combine multiple business lines spanning industries, geographies, or customer markets under a single parent company, the key to building a durable moat is having a central, leverageable core competency that can drive higher profits. This often happens when disparate businesses with similar technological underpinnings can leverage their investments in technology across multiple platforms, delivering new product developments at a lower average cost than pure-play competitors can. General Electric does this with its jet engines, gas turbines, and wind turbines; 3M has a pool of internally developed patents that it can transfer across product lines. More importantly, having integrated segments allows the firm to develop multiple distinct touch points with the customer, often tightening the customer relationship, leading to high switching costs. Over time, relationships are difficult to penetrate from the outside as the incumbent knows the customer well, and has developed a range of integrated products to address specific customer needs. As a result, customer retention rates and consumable revenues are key indicators for the strength of the moat in this category.

Key considerations for diversified industrials:

- Which, if any, segments are more valuable as a stand-alone entity? How does any one segment contribute to the company's collective competency?
- Is the company as active in divesting businesses as it is in acquiring?
- Inherent risk among diversified firms is acquisition valuation risk, because poor acquisitions absorb not only investor capital, but also management capacity.
- How does the firm choose its acquisition targets? How does the acquired entity add value to the acquirer or the acquirer to the target?

15

Technology

Welcome to the tech sector, where many a fortune has been made—and lost—in the blink of an eye. Memories of the late-1990s dot-com bubble and its dramatic burst in 2000–01 still loom large in the minds of many investors. Fueled by heady growth rates, speculation, overconfidence, and plenty of venture capital, tech stocks—especially those that had anything to do with the Internet—enjoyed meteoric rises followed by equally spectacular crashes just a few years later. Since then, many tech companies have risen from the ashes and soared to new heights.

Indeed, the tech sector is full of fast-moving, ever-changing companies, making it an exciting arena for investors. However, those very same traits also make the sector challenging territory for confidently predicting excess returns over the long term. That's why we think it's important to look at sustainable competitive advantages in addition to growth potential when looking for investment opportunities in technology. Of the 140 tech companies we currently cover, about 15% have wide moats—most of those occurring among software

Percentage of Companies per Rating   Prevalence of Moat Sources (%)

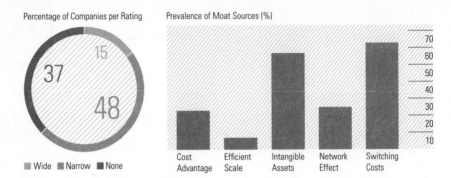

Figure 15.1   Economic Moat Characteristics of the Technology Sector
Source: Morningstar.

and semiconductor companies. The rest of the sector splits fairly evenly among no-moat and narrow-moat firms, with many of the narrow moats stemming from high customer switching costs and intangible assets, as well as other moat sources, as Figure 15.1 illustrates.

Consumer Technology

The consumer technology industry is home to some of the world's best-known brands, including Apple, Panasonic, Samsung, and many others. These firms are in the business of offering some combination of hardware, software, services, and content to a vast audience of users.

Switching costs are critical for any semblance of a moat in the consumer technology industry. Given extremely short product life cycles, the only consumer technology firms that can generate sustainable excess returns over time are those that can embed switching costs to ensure that today's customers will make repeat purchases tomorrow. Hardware firms may initially profit from the sale of a gadget, but it's the software, services, and content around that hardware that are likely to drive product purchases in the future. We believe consumer electronics hardware is relatively commoditized. The hardware specs of an iPhone, for example, have largely been matched by dozens of products in recent years, but we believe software, apps, and media content purchased by iPhone customers will help Apple retain a good portion of its user base in the years ahead.

Gaming firms can also develop competitive advantages from the intangible asset of intellectual property. Successful gaming companies have a track record of monetizing intellectual property year after year by delivering quality content in sequels and expansion packs for popular games. Although we see low barriers to entry in the gaming industry, leading gaming content companies should be able to live off the riches of a handful of extremely popular franchises for the next several years.

Because technologies change so fast and consumers are so fickle, it's extremely difficult for consumer tech firms to develop wide economic moats. Narrow moats are possible for firms that can secure cost advantages, customer switching costs, or, in gaming, long-term licenses of valuable intellectual property (IP). For example, Electronic Arts has dominated the sports video game market with brands like Madden, which has lasted 25 years, by licensing IP from the NFL and building software development engines that allow high-quality games to be made quickly, easily, and inexpensively. Outside of these factors, however, we have less certainty that any single consumer tech firm will generate outsize economic profits beyond the next decade, unless such firms expand beyond the consumer market and into the more stable business enterprise space.

Key considerations when studying consumer technology companies:

- What aspects of a company's products help it retain loyal users and drive future product sales? Think about the breadth and depth of the existing customer base and the willingness and ability to switch to a competing product or platform.
- What is the company's competitive position around software, services, and IP, and how has it evolved over time?
- Do the firm's products command a premium position in the marketplace? We would look for incremental signs of price erosion or support as one indication that a firm might be able to capture excess economic profits.
- Think about how a company's products can be replicated by substitutes. Can a user perform similar functions with a different or more integrated product, or would a user have to own multiple devices or platforms to perform all of the necessary functions or have a similar user experience?
- When looking at returns on invested capital, does a company benefit from outsourced manufacturing and a low fixed cost base?

Enterprise Hardware Systems

Enterprise hardware systems vendors sell equipment used to support IT and business operations, including computers, printers, phone systems, servers, data storage, and networking equipment.

These hardware vendors cannot rely much on intangible assets or cost advantages to build their moats, because enterprise technologies are easily replicated, customers are reasonably sophisticated, and barriers to entry are relatively low. Customer switching costs, however, can be a primary source of advantage for these companies, and vendors typically take three common approaches to increase the stickiness of their products. First, vendors build software content into their products. User interfaces, system management tools, analytics, and programming interfaces can increase the customer's perception of value and provide tighter integration into the customer's environment. Second, vendors try to lengthen life cycles of systems. Chassis/blade architectures are common, in which a customer can add or upgrade capacity by purchasing additional hardware modules without replacing an entire system. Additionally, vendors will typically provide software or processor upgrades that can be implemented with minimal operational disruption and at significantly lower cost than migrating to a competing platform. Third, vendors offer annual maintenance services that are usually priced at 10% to 20% of the initial price of the system in order to capture a high-margin stream of recurring revenue and remain relevant to the customer between product cycles.

Products that are tightly integrated and support mission-critical processes provide more durable competitive advantages. Business functions are usually supported by multiple systems tied together by hardware and software platforms, and vendors that supply products that cut across multiple points of integration are better positioned to sustain economic profits than those vendors that provide point solutions. For example, a cluster of core data-center switches that tie together database servers, application servers, and web servers is more difficult to abandon than a branch office router that supports a small, remote sales team. Similarly, products that support mission-critical processes are stickier than those that don't because the risk involved with migration typically outweighs perceived benefits. Finally, products that require significant expertise and training to configure and manage are typically stickier than those that are plug-and-play.

EMC is a good example of a company that has carved out an economic moat based on high switching costs. First, the large network storage company already has an extensive base of installed systems. Second, even a smaller challenger in possession of good technology may find it difficult to take share from EMC, as risk-averse chief information officers are unlikely to take a chance on an unproven new vendor without significant incentive. Third, as customers expand their storage environments, they can often leverage their existing software and pay only for additional hardware. Finally, EMC's broad product line provides flexibility, enabling customers to start with low-end gear and then move up the value chain as their data needs grow.

Key considerations for enterprise hardware systems:

- Deeply integrated products supporting mission-critical applications are stickiest. Do the vendor's products support mission-critical applications or point solutions? Are they firmly entrenched in a customer's environment or easily switched out (that is, commoditylike), and how costly is the migration?
- Faster product cycles provide competitors frequent opportunities to steal customers. What defenses has a vendor built to protect itself from competition throughout the product cycle? How easy is it for competitors to replicate the vendor's products? Do customers find value in new product features or are the products becoming increasingly commoditized with each product cycle?
- Stronger companies are typically on the "short list" of approved vendors, have deep reseller relationships, and have a strong direct salesforce and long-term relationships with key decision-makers. Is the vendor a trusted supplier to large enterprises?
- Most enterprise hardware systems vendors are active acquirers with significant excess cash balances, so it's appropriate to adjust return on invested capital (ROIC) calculations by subtracting excess cash from invested capital and including acquired goodwill.

IT Services

Despite a highly competitive and fragmented market, a number of large IT services firms have earned economic moats due to switching costs and intangible assets. Given the intimate and often mission-critical nature of work performed by IT service providers, such as technology consulting, systems integration, and custom application development, clients are often unwilling to switch vendors. In addition, an established relationship frequently enhances an IT service provider's insight into the client's operations and emerging technology trends that will most affect the client. We have seen this dynamic lead to decades-long relationships given the relevance and timeliness of solutions. A trusted IT service partner can also gain additional business via word of mouth, and brand is very important in this respect. A successful track record reinforces repeat business and ongoing, sticky relationships.

The size of a company's global delivery model can have a significant bearing on the scale and value of contracts it secures. There are only a few global players that can provide full end-to-end IT services solutions for the world's largest multinational corporations. The ability to change global processes in a fast and efficient manner generally translates into higher-end client engagement and better financial performance. At the other end of the spectrum, IT services companies that rely on business-process outsourcing and infrastructure outsourcing, which are easier to implement and don't carry meaningful switching costs, are exposed to commoditization from pure-play rivals.

It's tough for IT services companies to earn wide moats. Although we believe these services and leading companies will be around for the long haul, it's often difficult to project how valuable these services will be for corporations more than 10 years into the future, which raises questions about long-term pricing power. Additionally, these service businesses are affected by changes in technology, and disruption is always possible.

That said, Accenture is one IT service provider that we recently upgraded to wide-moat status, based on its customer switching costs and intangible assets. Deep and broad industry expertise, a global delivery network, and satisfied customer references have provided the company with a successful foundation in the highly competitive and fragmented IT services industry. Accenture's global nature sets the company apart from smaller rivals, and allows it to draw from a vast pool of specialist personnel and technology tools. Another critical component of Accenture's success has been its ability to attract and foster close and long-lasting business relationships. The stickiness of these relationships is made evident by the fact that, as of mid-2013, 99 of the company's largest 100 clients (by revenue) had been with the firm for at least five years, and 92 had been with the firm for at least 10 years. These figures highlight the intimate and often mission-critical nature of Accenture's work, which makes clients unwilling to switch between service providers.

Key considerations for enterprise services companies:

- How broad and deep is the company's global delivery model? Can the business offer services on a scale that others can't? It's good to have a comprehensive portfolio that is capable of offering a one-stop-shop.
- When evaluating IT service providers, focus on the depth and longevity of existing client relationships. Depth can be measured by looking at the trends in revenue generated from the top five to 10 accounts, while longevity can be assessed by looking at the length of these relationships.
- Where in the value chain does the company play? Can it offer the higher-value consulting and integration services, while keeping up with new and emerging technology trends? Or are they facing commoditization in lower-end outsourcing services? Look to the company's profitability and return-based metrics for insight on its ability to charge premium prices.
- Even if a company meets the qualitative criteria for an economic moat—such as switching costs and intangible assets—it's important to have confidence in the firm's ability to generate positive economic profits. For IT services firms, repeated execution issues may prevent the company from turning out positive economic profits.

Semiconductors

This category includes companies in the semiconductor supply chain, from suppliers of manufacturing equipment and raw materials, to firms that design and manufacture chip devices. The central driver of the semiconductor industry is its ability to innovate so that computing power increases while the costs of that computing power rapidly decrease—commonly referred to as *Moore's Law*.

Cost advantages and intangible assets are common sources of moats in the semiconductor space. Often, companies that have leading share in their respective market segments benefit from economies of scale, resulting in moats based on cost advantages. By taking advantage of a lead in market share and scale, firms can spread out their costs more effectively on a per-unit basis, enabling them to invest more heavily in R&D than competitors, which in turn allows them to remain at the technology forefront and create barriers to entry.

Intangible assets, such as superior chip-design expertise and intellectual capital, also contribute to moats for analog chipmakers, particularly those with outstanding records of innovation and successful products, such as Linear

Technology and Maxim Integrated. Analog chips are highly proprietary, so they lack direct substitutes, and the engineers who design these products face a set of unique design challenges. As a result, firms that have years of R&D and manufacturing experience and that can retain significant analog engineering talent (which is scarce) are likely to earn excess profits over time and be candidates for moat ratings. It is rare for technology patents to result in moats because of the common practice of cross-licensing and use of standards in the industry, which serve to level the patent playing field. There are a few exceptions, such as Qualcomm's patents surrounding CDMA wireless technology, which generates royalties on every 3G and 4G handset sold.

Determining the width of a specific semiconductor company's moat isn't easy, because of the constant technological changes in the industry. Instead, the difference between a narrow and wide moat rating is often determined by the competitive dynamics of the specific product subcategory. Certain products in the semiconductor industry, such as computer processors, are more proprietary, while others such as memory chips are more commoditylike in nature. All else equal, segments that involve more complex products tend to have wide moats, as the technical challenges of replicating products create high barriers to entry. On the other hand, firms that have less technically sophisticated products tend to have either a narrow or no-moat rating.

Semiconductor giant Intel boasts a wide economic moat, thanks to its immense scale, which gives the firm long-term advantages in maintaining its lead in the microprocessor market. Intel holds the edge in terms of processor performance because of its massive R&D budget, which is unmatched in the semiconductor industry. In addition, the firm has the resources to continually invest in the most cutting-edge semiconductor manufacturing technologies. By having a one- to two-year lead over the rest of the chip industry in driving Moore's Law, Intel has the ability to produce chips that are faster or more power-efficient, or both, at a lower per-unit cost than any other chipmaker.

Key considerations for semiconductor companies:

- Does the company have leading market share in its segment of the semiconductor industry? Can it stay ahead of the technology curve by spending more on R&D than competitors do?
- Does the firm have superior engineering talent (especially important in the analog chip segment) or technology patents that allow it to achieve excess returns on capital for an extended period of time? How difficult is it for a

competitor to come out with a product that is competitive from a technological and pricing standpoint?

- Has the firm been gaining or losing market share in recent periods because
  of a technology shift? Is the gain or loss short term or permanent?
- Investors should analyze returns on capital and profitability over entire
  business cycles, which typically last three to five years. The semiconductor
  industry is highly cyclical, so excess returns during business upturns may
  not necessarily mean that a firm can generate excess returns on average
  over an entire cycle.
- What are the reinvestment needs of chipmakers in terms of ongoing R&D
  and capital expenditures? Analog chipmakers, in particular, benefit from
  stable pricing but also do not rely on cutting-edge manufacturing techniques that require hefty ongoing investments.

Software

Software firms create, sell, and maintain programs written for mainframes,
servers, computers, and other computing devices, to help run the device or help
the user accomplish a task. Software can be sold as a product (license) or as a
service (Software as a Service, or SaaS). Software companies tend to fall into
two main categories: infrastructure and application.

Network effect is a main source of economic moats for some software
companies. The more users a brand of application software generates, the
larger the network effect as the user base settles on a de facto industry standard. Think Microsoft Office or Adobe Photoshop.

Infrastructure software companies can also generate excess economic
returns from high switching costs. Mission-critical infrastructure software that
requires significant customization, implementation, and training will have significant switching costs for customers. By embedding itself into mission-critical
customer workflows, an infrastructure software firm can create significant barriers that dissuade customers from considering replacements. As a result, software firms can see high renewal rates, creating an annuitylike revenue stream.

For software firms providing software as a service, economies of scale are
another important consideration for competitive advantage. Given the high capital outlays for these businesses and the lower-priced subscription model (relative to perpetual-license models), economies of scale are necessary to generate

returns on capital. Firms without necessary capital resources are unable to successfully compete in this industry segment. Intangible assets including intellectual property and government regulations serve as another source of economic moat for software companies.

Software companies that have significant market share and enjoy large network effects will likely generate excess economic returns over a long period of time. Narrow-moat firms typically have products with meaningful market share and switching costs, but may not be the market-share leader. Additionally, narrow-moat firms may have a strong market position in a point solution or one piece of the software environment, but they may be less integrated into the entire software architecture. In contrast, wide-moat firms may have near-monopoly market-share status, with a product (or products) considered to be the industry or category standard. Because of the fast pace of change in the software industry, firms run the risk of obsolescence as newcomers and rivals attempt to gain a competitive advantage. Defending a product from competitors while ignoring new trends is a common miscalculation for software firms. Incumbents must continue to innovate or pursue an M&A strategy to keep abreast of industry and market changes.

Intuit is one well-known software firm that boasts a wide moat, underpinned by high switching costs and positive network effects. Learning to use its accounting, tax, and personal finance applications takes some time and effort. Therefore, users would not only incur additional software and training costs, but would also face operational disruption and the risk of errors in transferring financial information if they were to switch to an alternative product or competing application. To strengthen the stickiness of its products, Intuit has skillfully intertwined the functionality between its multiple products, making users of one of the firm's applications more likely to adopt an additional product as their needs expand. For instance, QuickBooks users are likely to adopt Intuit's payments and payroll services, and Quicken users are more easily lured into transferring their year-long financial information into TurboTax. Furthermore, the pervasiveness of Intuit's applications generates positive network effects because the commanding market share of its products provides a strong and self-reinforcing incentive for accountants and end users to look to Intuit's applications.

Key considerations for software companies:

- The deeper software is embedded into a customer's mission-critical business functions, the higher the switching costs are. Does the application require extensive implementation or customization? Is it more expensive in capital or other resources to replace the incumbent software than to keep paying maintenance or subscription fees?

- Are there network effects created by users or developers of the software? Do users choose a particular software product to ensure the most compatibility? Do developers develop for an application or platform because it has the most users and therefore has the largest potential market?
- Economies of scale are an important consideration, as many software companies begin providing their software products as services. Cloud-based computing, infrastructure as a service, and platform as a service each require significant initial and ongoing capital outlays for building and operating data centers. These costs may be prohibitive for smaller participants and those lacking a customer base large enough to offset the startup costs.
- Does the firm own patents, intellectual property, or brands that give its products an advantage in the marketplace?

Telecom Services

Telecommunication carriers provide services such as wireless telephony, fixed-line telephony, short message services, and Internet data access. Most large companies offer customers all services. Many telephone carriers were once government agencies or privately owned, state-regulated monopolies. Rapidly maturing markets and the competition to retain customers demonstrate the importance of economic moats in this sector.

The quality and size of a company's network can drive cost advantages in the telecom industry. For example, in the United States, cable networks are the only facilities currently capable of providing phone, TV, and Internet access—a quality advantage that has allowed cable firms to steadily gain market share of overall telecom spending. In addition, as wireless data gains importance, the spectrum needed to provide network capacity has become an increasingly scarce and unique intangible asset. Scale—in terms of subscribers and infrastructure—is critical to efficiently deploying new network technology, minimizing per-customer marketing costs, gaining access to new devices, and generally spreading overhead costs across as large a customer base as possible. Also, the more subscribers a firm has on its own network, the less it's forced to pay interconnection fees to other carriers.

Understanding the competitive landscape and regulatory backdrop of a specific market is essential when assessing moats of individual companies. The number of players in a given market serves as a useful guide to the competitive intensity. Wireless markets with three or fewer players, and fixed-line markets with two or fewer, tend to be much more rational than those with more and allow firms to generate efficient scale and earn strong returns on invested capital. It's also important to consider the regulatory environment, as an unfriendly one can prohibit an otherwise solid company from enjoying sustainable cost advantages. The U.K., for example, has witnessed some of the most aggressive regulation in the world, with the forced split of incumbent BT Group into retail and wholesale units. The move allowed dozens of competitors into the fixed-line market. Mexico, meanwhile, recently adopted a new antitrust reform act that threatens America Movil's cost advantage because the firm will likely have to pay higher interconnection rates than its peers. Other regulatory actions that threaten telecom profitability include price setting, forced universal service, and the creation of municipally funded rivals.

The rapid technological change in the industry, persistent threat of government intervention, and massive capital requirements of this business prevent us from assigning wide moats to any of the telecom companies we cover. But many firms do earn narrow moats, primarily due to cost advantages.

Other key considerations for evaluating telecom companies:

- What is the outlook for customer acquisition and retention spending in the firm's specific subsector?
- It's important to know whether a company's strategy and those of its rivals are more focused on market share or profitability.
- What are the realistic chances for carrier consolidation or expansion in the company's market (or markets)? Gauging whether a sector is more likely to expand or contract is key when analyzing a firm's long-term competitive advantage.
- Given the increasing proliferation of smartphones, a wireless carrier's device portfolio can be a differentiator when you are evaluating the firm's competitive advantages.
- Analyzing a firm's—and a sector's—trend in the average margin per user, or AMPU (operating income divided by subscribers), can give an accurate gauge of whether the cost-advantage moat source is strengthening or eroding.

16

Utilities

The key differentiating factor for utilities' economic moats is the extent to which the utilities' businesses are regulated or deregulated.

Regulated utilities—companies like Duke Energy and Southern Company—generally own difficult-to-replicate distribution, transmission, and generation networks that produce and deliver energy sources such as electricity, natural gas, propane, or water. State and federal regulators control pricing and returns for these utilities in an effort to keep consumer costs low while still enabling decent returns for capital providers. As a result, these companies usually earn at least their costs of capital in the long run, creating positive, if moderate, returns and narrow moats for many regulated utilities.

Nonregulated independent power producers, or IPPs, are much different from regulated utilities. IPPs own power plants that use enriched uranium, fossil fuels, or renewable energy to generate electricity for sale in wholesale markets or through bilateral agreements with distributors. Earnings typically are volatile, cyclical, and closely tied to energy commodity markets, making sustained

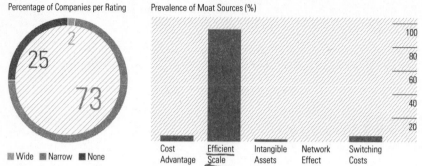

Percentage of Companies per Rating   Prevalence of Moat Sources (%)

■ Wide   ■ Narrow   ■ None

Figure 16.1   Economic Moat Characteristics of the Utilities Sector
Source: Morningstar.

competitive advantages and economic moats less likely. Only firms with clear cost advantages—often those focused on nuclear energy rather than fossil fuels or renewable energy—have a shot at creating moats. See Figure 16.1 for an illustration of the moat ratings and sources found in the utilities sector.

Regulated and Diversified Utilities

For regulated utilities, efficient scale is clearly the primary source of moat. State and federal regulators typically grant utilities exclusive rights to operate as service-territory monopolies. In exchange for these rights, regulators set prices at levels that aim to minimize customer costs while still allowing fair returns for the utilities' capital providers.

This implicit contract between regulators and capital providers should, on balance, allow regulated utilities to achieve at least their costs of capital over time, though short-term returns can vary based on demand trends, investment cycles, operating costs, and access to financing. Intuitively, these utilities should all have economic moats based on efficient scale, but there can be situations where aggressive regulation offsets this advantage, limiting excess returns on capital. This risk of adverse regulatory decisions prevents most regulated utilities from earning wide moat ratings. But because the threat of material value destruction is low, and normalized returns do exceed costs of capital in most cases, we're comfortable assigning narrow moat ratings to most regulated utilities.

Diversified utilities, which can own a mix of regulated and nonregulated assets, have a chance to establish wide moats if their nonregulated businesses can demonstrate sustainable cost advantages. In the wholesale power markets, we consider nuclear power generation the only energy source that can sustain a long-term cost advantage and thus generate a wide moat. Nuclear power plants' high capital costs deter new entrants, and their low variable costs give them an edge over competing fossil-fuel power producers.

Exelon is a diversified utility whose different lines of business have different moat characteristics, but it's one of the only utilities to earn a wide moat rating overall, thanks to its position as the leading nuclear power producer in the United States. As mentioned earlier, nuclear operators like Exelon have two primary competitive advantages. First, nuclear plants take years to site and build, cost several billion dollars, and often face community opposition. These are significant barriers to entry, giving operators an effective low-cost monopoly in a given region. Second, no other reliable power generation source can match the cost or scale of a nuclear plant. Nuclear plants' low variable costs and low greenhouse gas emissions—relative to competing fossil-fuel power generation sources like coal and natural gas—reduce substitution threats. As long as electricity remains a critical energy source in the U.S., nuclear plants should maintain a substantial low-cost advantage and generate high returns on capital.

Meanwhile, we believe Exelon's regulated distribution utilities deserve narrow moats, based on their regulated return levels. Exelon's retail supply business, on the other hand, has no economic moat. Retail power and gas markets are highly competitive with virtually no barriers to entry, switching costs, or product differentiation. Although customers are sticky, retailers mostly end up competing on price.

Key considerations to keep in mind when analyzing regulated utilities:

- Cost-of-service ratemaking supports narrow moats for regulated utilities. Regulators must allow a reasonable opportunity for a utility to recover its operating and capital costs through customer rates to support a narrow moat. See that investment needs, cost inflation, and demand are aligned.
- Is the utility earning near its regulatory allowed return? A wide divergence between the allowed returns that regulators use to set utilities' rates and the utilities' earned returns typically leads to rate increases or rate cuts to bring earned returns in line with allowed returns.

- A diversified utility's nonregulated assets might strengthen or weaken its moat. For nonregulated energy businesses, look primarily for cost advantages or barriers to entry. The more capital a utility deploys in nonregulated assets, the wider cost advantages it must achieve to earn economic profits.

Independent Power Producers

Independent power producers generally have a hard time establishing sustainable competitive advantages because they are price takers that operate in commodity energy markets. IPPs' returns on capital depend on the relationship between commodity fuel costs, market competition, and regional energy demand, limiting opportunities to establish long-term economic moats. That said, low-cost nuclear, coal, and renewable-energy power producers have the best chance to establish competitive advantages if they operate in markets with higher-cost competitors. Even so, keep in mind that low-cost generation sources typically require large capital investments and must earn high returns for many years to produce economic profits. Barriers to entry can be another near-term source of competitive advantage for IPPs, given the large sums of time and money it usually takes to win regulatory approvals, find a suitable site, and complete construction on a new power plant.

Ormat Technologies, a renewable-energy company focused on geothermal power, is one of the few IPPs that has been able to carve out a competitive advantage and earn a narrow moat. For starters, Ormat's geothermal plants run more frequently than intermittent wind and solar sources do, with the highest availability of any renewable resource. Moreover, Ormat has stable, long-term power purchase agreements covering all of its geothermal output and virtually no variable fuel costs, which ensure the company a certain return on capital for many years. As one of the most experienced geothermal players in the world, on both the products and the operations side, Ormat has a decades-long head start over potential competitors in power-plant design, though large industrial players could make a strong move into the business if demand for geothermal continues to grow.

Key considerations for evaluating independent power producers:

- Unlike most other energy sources, electricity is not fungible. This limits supply in a given region and can result in stronger or weaker competitive advantages. It's important to consider competitors' generation costs and barriers to entry in the region where a power producer operates.

- Watch for market-distorting public policies. Government incentives for renewable energy are eroding competitive advantages for nuclear and fossil-fuel power producers, while environmental regulation aimed at fossil-fuel power plants is strengthening competitive advantages for cleaner nuclear and renewable energy.
- New-build economics depend on the relationship between projected capital costs and variable costs. Capital-intensive nuclear and renewable energy has low variable costs and higher profits. Fossil-fuel power plants typically are cheaper to build but have higher variable costs and lower profits.

About the Authors

Heather Brilliant, CFA, is co-chief executive officer of Morningstar Australasia. Before assuming this role in 2014, Brilliant was global director of equity and corporate credit research for seven years. In this role, she led Morningstar's global equity and corporate credit research teams, consisting of more than 120 analysts, strategists, and directors. She also served on Morningstar's Economic Moat committee, a group of senior members of the equity research team responsible for reviewing all of the firm's Economic Moat and Moat Trend ratings.

Before joining Morningstar in 2003 as an equity analyst, Brilliant spent several years as an equity research analyst for boutique investment firms. She has covered a variety of sectors, including pharmaceuticals, biotechnology, business services, and retail. She started her finance career at Bank of America as a corporate finance analyst, covering the auto industry.

Brilliant holds a bachelor's degree in economics from Northwestern University and a master's degree in business administration from the University of Chicago Booth School of Business. She also holds the Chartered Financial Analyst® designation. Brilliant is a member of the CFA Institute Board of Governors and is a past chairman of the CFA Society of Chicago.

Elizabeth Collins, CFA, is director of equity research, North America for Morningstar, responsible for leading the firm's team of North American-based equity research analysts. Before assuming her current role in 2014, Collins was chair of Morningstar's Economic Moat committee, a group of senior members of the equity research team responsible for reviewing all Economic Moat and Moat Trend ratings issued by Morningstar. She was also director of basic materials equity research, where she oversaw coverage of companies in the agriculture, building materials, chemicals, coal, forest products, metals and mining, packaging, and steel industries. Prior to leading the basic materials team, Collins was a senior analyst on the energy team. She joined Morningstar in 2005.

Collins holds a bachelor's degree in psychology from Boston College and a master's degree in business administration from DePaul University. She also holds the Chartered Financial Analyst® designation.

Joel Bloomer is head of Asia-Pacific equity and credit research for Morningstar. He is responsible for developing high-quality, independent, and fundamental research in the region and serves as a member of Morningstar's Economic Moat committee. Before assuming his current role, Bloomer helped start an equity management boutique in South Africa, where he held several research and business leadership. Earlier in his career, Bloomer held a variety of positions with Morningstar in Chicago, including head of consumer equity research, senior real estate services and investment trust analyst, and generalist.

Bloomer holds a bachelor's degree in finance and economics from the University of Illinois.

Matthew Coffina, CFA, is editor of *Morningstar® StockInvestor*SM, Morningstar's flagship stocks newsletter. Coffina manages the publication's two real-money, market-beating model portfolios, the Tortoise and the Hare, which focus on investing in companies with strong and growing competitive advantages trading at discounts to their intrinsic values. Coffina joined Morningstar in 2007 and previously served as a senior equity analyst covering healthcare services companies. He designed the discounted cash-flow model used by Morningstar's analysts to assign fair value estimates to more than 1,500 global companies. Coffina holds a bachelor's degree in economics from Oberlin College and the Chartered Financial Analyst® designation.

Stephen Ellis is director of financial services research for Morningstar, overseeing equity and credit coverage of companies in the financial services industry. Ellis is also a member of Morningstar's Economic Moat committee, a group of senior members of the equity research team responsible for reviewing all economic moat and moat trend ratings issued by Morningstar. He is also a former editor of the *Morningstar® Opportunistic Investor*^{SM} newsletter.

Ellis holds bachelor's and master's degrees in business administration from the University of Redlands, where he graduated cum laude and with departmental honors.

Gareth James is head of Asia-Pacific training and operations for Morningstar. James is responsible for the quality of the research output of the Asia-Pacific equity and credit research team, including regional coverage universe optimization, project management, and platform coordination. He is also a member of Morningstar's Economic Moat, Global Valuation, and Australian Investment committees and co-manages the Australian Income Equities and Smallcap Equities portfolios.

James holds a bachelor's degree in physics from Kings College, University of London.

Warren Miller, CFA, is vice president of global quantitative research for Morningstar. He leads the firm's quantitative research team to create analytically rigorous tools and methodologies for investors. In addition, he manages Morningstar's Conviction Long portfolio, an equity investment strategy geared toward institutional investors, and he led the development of Morningstar's Quantitative Equity Ratings. Miller holds a bachelor's degree in industrial engineering and economics from Northwestern University and a master's degree in business administration from the University of Chicago Booth School of Business. He also holds the Chartered Financial Analyst® designation.

Josh Peters, CFA, is the director of equity-income strategy for Morningstar and editor of the monthly newsletter *Morningstar® DividendInvestor*^{SM}. As part of his role as editor, he manages the newsletter's Builder and Harvest Portfolios, composed of individual stocks targeted to generate above-average income and superior total returns. Peters is also the author of *The Ultimate Dividend Playbook: Income, Insight, and Independence for Today's Investor*, published by John Wiley & Sons in 2008. Peters holds a bachelor's degree in history and economics from the University of Minnesota, Duluth. He also holds the Chartered Financial Analyst® designation.

Todd Wenning is an equity analyst for Morningstar, covering paper and packaging, engineering and construction, and chemical companies. He leads Morningstar's stewardship methodology and writes a monthly column on small-cap stocks for Morningstar.com®. Wenning holds a bachelor's degree in history from St. Joseph's University, where he graduated cum laude. At the time of publication, Todd is a Level III candidate for the Chartered Financial Analyst® designation.

Index